TRAVELLING IN AMHERST

TRAVELLING IN AMHERST

A POET'S JOURNAL

1931–1954

Robert Francis

Rowan Tree Press
Boston, Massachusetts
1986

Copyright © 1986, by Robert Francis

All rights reserved

Library of Congress Catalog Card Number 85-062398

ISBN 0-937672-19-x

Printed in the United States of America

ACKNOWLEDGMENTS

Cover illustration, aquatint by Abner Reed, 1810
Back cover photograph, courtesy of the Jones Library, Amherst, MA
Book design by Lazarillo

Poems: *Monadnock*, and *Hallelujah: A Sestina* are reprinted with permission, from THE ORB WEAVER, by Robert Francis, Wesleyan University Press, 1960; *Bronze, Old Man Feeding Hens, The Sound I Listened For, Squash in Blossom, Monadnock, Portrait, Hallelujah: A Sestina* are reprinted with permission, from ROBERT FRANCIS COLLECTED POEMS 1936–1976, University of Massachusetts Press, Amherst, MA, 1976.

Journal entries for November 21, 1933; June 11, 1934; May 22, 1950; and October 26, 1952 were published originally in FROST: A TIME TO TALK: CONVERSATIONS AND INDISCRETIONS RECORDED BY ROBERT FRANCIS, University of Massachusetts Press, Amherst, MA, © 1972, by Robert Francis.

Grateful acknowledgment for assistance in preparing this book to the Librarians of the Jones Library, and to Linda Seidman, of Archives and Manuscripts, the University of Massachusetts Library, Amherst, MA.

Rowan Tree Press
124 Chestnut Street
Boston, Massachusetts 02108

NOTE

Our intent in editing Robert Francis' Journal was to focus clearly the narrative of his growth as a poet. We have chosen this selection of entries from the day by day "uncertainty and suspense" of three decades of recorded experience to bring out the turning points or epiphanies of a life dedicated to writing poetry.

Some of the accounts of everyday experience, though absorbing in themselves, are not directly relevant to the story we are tracing, and have been omitted. Yet, aware of how interconnected all Francis' experience has been, we have kept many entries describing country walks, visits with neighbors, community occasions, for what they tell of the life from which his poems sprang.

Conversations with Robert Frost comprise not just an early chapter, but a salient theme of Francis' Journal. After each meeting, he would write down what they had discussed, recalling the words as exactly as he could. But because these talks have been published as a book in their own right, *Frost: A Time To Talk: Conversations and Indiscretions Recorded by Robert Francis,* only a few have been retained in this Journal to suggest the whole vital exchange between the poets.

INTRODUCTION

Early in our friendship, I remember telling Robert Francis that I wished we had been born at the same time so we could have experienced our youth together. Now, reading this Journal for the first time, I can be more sure that I would have enjoyed him in this earlier period.

Frankly, he is even better than I had imagined. One sees his sensitivity, for example, in his reaction to a neighbor perched in an apple tree, pruning and singing; his wisdom, as he considers the importance for human beings to change and continue changing; his ability to observe and record, as in his concise and charming description of Irish author James Stephens; and, beginning with the very first entry, his profound delight in writing poetry. In effect, with a sense of being there, one is privy to his development into a student of nature and human beings, a philosopher and a man of independence. And most clearly and often, of course, one sees the poet in progress, the man becoming the artist.

I have read Francis in several different forms: his poetry, fiction, essays, letters, autobiography, and now this Journal. Compelled to choose among them, I would favor his poetry and the Journal, the one for its truth, the other for its truest Francis.

Interestingly, had I access to the Journal before I met Francis in March, 1948, I probably would not have initiated the contact that would lead to our friendship—or at least not when I did. As co-editor of a brand-new, very modest poetry magazine in Northampton, Massachusetts, I wrote to him in nearby Amherst, inviting him to contribute some poems to its pages. It was

Introduction

"a good cause," I insisted in my letter to him, noting sheepishly that payment would consist of free copies of the magazine.

He responded by listing five "possible misinterpretations" that he might open himself to by making such a contribution, including the one that he was not able to sell his poetry; but he didn't say no. Rather, he threw the ball back: "I should sincerely welcome hearing your evidence that your cause is not only worthy but worthwhile," he wrote. I phoned him, accepted the challenge, and, several days later, he met me in his 1931 Chevrolet at the Amherst Common bus stop.

Although I could not have known, it was probably the worst time to be asking Francis for free poems, especially for such an unsophisticated publication with a circulation of less than 500. In addition to the fact that he depended on the sale of his poems for part of his livelihood, he was already in the most severe crisis of his writing career: a 16-year hiatus, begun in 1944, in which he did not have a single book of poems accepted by a publisher and suffered long periods without even magazine acceptances; a time in which he seriously questioned his ability to continue as a poet.

But there was no telling this from Francis' demeanor during that first visit or, for that matter, during any of our scores of visits or hundreds of letters exchanged before his publication dearth ended in 1960. The tall, slender, 46-year-old man I met that spring afternoon was hardly a picture of despair. What he was, most noticeably, was quiet: quietly gracious, witty, observant, curious. As we sat by the fireplace in his small, one-bedroom country house called Fort Juniper, or ate the fried parsnips and maple syrup supper, or walked along the tree-lined road in the dark evening, quietly he spoke of chickadees, poetry, moderation, Plato, his vegetable garden. He treated them all with a kind of authority that nevertheless invited participa-

Introduction

tion—first leading with a tentative-sounding observation, then inviting my opinion; so I was given the feeling that I was conversing as his equal. It was an approach that helped put at ease a 19-year-old reporter and aspiring poet who had known other writers only through brief discussions or interviews. It also suggested, though I was too self-conscious to think it at the time, that he had an uncommon sympathy for uneasy people.

My strong impression, when we parted that evening, was that this man who had produced three volumes of poetry and was awaiting the publication of his first novella was living the good and enviable life of a successful, full-time writer.

A close and lifelong friendship began that day, but I would not fully grasp the writing difficulty he was weathering until he was 70 years old and I read his just-published autobiography, THE TROUBLE WITH FRANCIS. Not that he hadn't referred occasionally during the intervening years to his creative dry spells or rejection slips, but these obstacles were always philosophically couched; they never smacked of crisis or anguish or anything extreme. To the contrary. By mentioning a disappointment, then observing that adversity was healthy for the soul, that it contained opportunities for growth if one sought them out, he left me mainly with the feeling of admiration for his wisdom and fortitude.

As his autobiography made clear, the life he had been living so stoically was far more difficult and complicated than even his best friends knew. Not only had he wanted "to crawl into a corner out of sight . . . shrink into my psychic shell" during the worst part of his publishing impasse, but also his extreme timidity in childhood, lingering into adulthood, had rendered him "incapable of accepting rude circumstances and small inconveniences" and of initiating friendships; he left teaching high school in Amherst after the first year because he found the

Introduction

students as a group "an unlovable mob;" at the age of 60 he participated in his first and only overt "love relation" and, in what he considered "perhaps the only shocking confession" of the book, declared he disliked, even detested, poetry.

But THE TROUBLE WITH FRANCIS was not sensational. In its low-keyed telling, it was a dense mix of homely detail and frank admission that provided an absorbing story of a life. And for those of us who knew Francis as one who almost never uttered a confessional word, it was also something of a surprise. Most of us who thought we knew him, knew him better and admired him even more after that book. So, apparently, did the critics. *Poetry* magazine's reviewer, for example, said it was "worthy in its modest way, to be set beside the autobiographies of Yeats and Edwin Muir." As for myself, after getting over a brief period of guilt at not having been better attuned to the inner Francis, I felt relief and gratitude that in the process of saying who he was, he had finally unburdened himself of so many self-imposed, painful constraints.

The almost compulsive candor running through the book could not have come into being lightly. Before Francis could be ready and able to write such an autobiography he had to move through a long, arduous time of growth, to overcome both his longstanding diffidence and the stoicism that enjoined him to suffer silently. And what makes TRAVELLING IN AMHERST particularly interesting and a valuable complement to his autobiography is its deeply honest, present tense description of the very years, 1931–54, in which much of this growth occurred. Indeed, the struggle that took place during this period was what assured his achievement both as a man and as a poet.

It deepened my interest in the Journal to keep in mind Francis' circumstances when he was writing it. His situation at the

x

Introduction

outset of TRAVELLING IN AMHERST seems, in retrospect, like the setting for a drama with an unpromising outcome. There he was, a shy man with a degree in education from Harvard, who had turned his back on the social and competitive world he had no heart for, now trying for the fourth year to make a career as a writer, with no book published or in sight, still earning most of his income by playing and teaching violin, and still, at the age of 29, living with his stepmother and Baptist minister-father.

How did he manage to liberate himself and develop into the man who is now 85 and has written some of the better poetry produced in the United States?

For one thing, he left the parental roof when he was 30. It was a small move geographically. It simply put him closer to the center of town and within a shorter walking distance of his violin pupils. But as a fundamental step toward independence and identity, it began forcing his growth. In the next eight years, moving from one rented residence to another in Amherst, he began learning how to economize. It was helpful preparation for a life that would almost always be lived at a near-subsistence level, but it was also more or less a natural response to his personal priorities. If he had been late in leaving home, he was not so late in understanding that material possessions were not what he wanted for himself, but rather the power to think, write, read, to walk through woods and meadows when he wanted to—which also meant meeting people only when he chose. He was after a life on his own terms, based on his needs and what he thought were his resources.

Though he tried avoiding people much of the time, living in apartment houses in the center of town made that difficult. One of his four landladies made it almost impossible. Margaret Sutton Briscoe Hopkins, his landlady for more than two years, was

Introduction

a strong-willed, outspoken woman of many talents and interests who insisted that Francis become more worldly and self-confident. It seems that the "redoubtable" Mrs. Hopkins may have given him his first important opportunity to assert his own will in the interest of keeping his integrity intact; indeed, that the process helped him to define what it was he wanted to keep intact. In his Journal he writes: "She has helped me by rubbing my fur the wrong way and thus sharpening my awareness of myself." And in his autobiography, describing the relationship as "a true symbiosis," he acknowledges that when it was over "she had bidden me to be a man and had helped me to become a little more of one than I had been."

She did one more thing. Presumably she believed that getting her unassertive tenant together with supremely confident Robert Frost would spark Francis to audacity and gumption, so she took it upon herself to introduce them. Doing so, she initiated one of the key relationships in Francis' life and one that he might not have sought himself.

From their first meeting in 1933, when Frost became a full-time Amherst resident until his death thirty years later, that relationship had a largely salutary effect on Francis. The famous Pulitzer Prize-winning poet, 27 years older than Francis, filled the traditional role of guiding and encouraging mentor, at a time when the younger poet badly needed one.

Frost spurred Francis to work at his poetry with new confidence, and as the poet became more sure, so did the man, albeit slowly. During this time of being newly on his own, he also found additional confidence through his own resourcefulness as he tried increasingly to make the best of everything he had. It became virtually an art that he perfected in a very conscious way. He not only used it—was compelled to use it—in managing the little money he made and, later, in preparing his meals

Introduction

from herbs and vegetables he raised; he applied it to his whole life, including his writing, which explains why his life and poetry were so closely intertwined. Moreover, to this resourcefulness he brought discipline and balance, qualities that were already critical elements of his philosophy.

To what extent this way of life was attributable to his having been the dutiful son of a Baptist minister or to his admiration for Emerson and Thoreau, among others, I have no idea. It seems clear, however, that his moral and philosophical views were being seriously shaped and reshaped as he tried his wings for the first time.

These views seldom lacked tests of their durability, not even in periods of success. The publication of his first book, STAND WITH ME HERE, took place when he was 35, ten years after his decision to become a writer. And two years later his second book, VALHALLA AND OTHER POEMS appeared. But there was a strange, unfortunate irony about it all. Even as Frost praised him—"I am swept off my feet by the goodness of your poems . . ."—a number of critics were noting that some of Francis' poetry sounded too much like Frost's. It was a charge that trailed Francis for decades, even though any basis for it had disappeared as early as VALHALLA. Predictably, I never heard Francis complain about it, and while it must have bothered him to some degree, it's my guess that he acknowledged to himself having briefly borrowed a bit of Frost's technique, but then used the criticism as a prod to become more genuinely Francis. Certainly dark brooding about it would not have been his style; he'd find it too negative, too unproductive to become anxiety-ridden about whether the comparison with Frost would dim the critics' enthusiasm for his future work, and whether that would mean a dimming of his chances with publishers. Which, of course, it did.

Introduction

There is a strong positiveness running through Francis' mind which, while balanced by a real sense of the negative, he clearly prefers in the interest of being happy and productive. If he is philosophically grave over the evil he sees in a spider killing a grasshopper, as he tells us in his poem, "The Orb Weaver," he is cheered by the fact that cows can eat poison ivy and turn it into wholesome milk. The skillful trick, he might say, is to look at a negative thing and find its own natural, inherent contradictions. When his father died in 1940, he tried to see the positive aspects of his death: that he had died without pain and in the company of people he most loved, that he had received the best nursing care. But all of that couldn't diminish the loss of a beloved man who was also the last member of his immediate family. Or the loss, either, of what he still perceived as his true home.

What he could and did do, however, was typical: with the $1,000 from his father's life insurance, he had his own home built. At 39, when he moved into Fort Juniper, he carried with him a sense of profound loss that was partially balanced by a new and profound sense of well-being. He finally had what he had dreamed of for years: a place of his own, surrounded by woods, fields and a stream, the solitude for writing and thinking.

Unhappily, the pleasures of Fort Juniper were soon interrupted. World War II came, and Francis, a pacifist, registered as a non-combatant. He was drafted when he was 40 and did not return to his Fort until almost two and a half years later.

Perhaps because of my own military experience and my distaste for much of it, I marvel at his performance under the U.S. Government. He spent only four months in uniform; for the rest, because of his age, he worked on chicken farms and taught in classrooms. Still—this quiet man actually drilling a

Introduction

squad in basic training? Beheading a chicken? And how did he adapt so flexibly to the loss of so much of his personal freedom, a freedom he had won by forsaking the teaching profession? Sometimes, I remind myself, to know Francis is to underestimate him, or rather to underestimate his remarkable resourcefulness.

Some years later, remembering his own military time, he wrote to me: "If you are drafted, do not think of it as the end of living. It will be a hard time and a delicate time for you, but it may mean, it could easily mean, a new moult."

It definitely meant a new moult and further "coming out of himself," as he put it, for Francis. When he returned to Fort Juniper, one more volume of poetry, THE SOUND I LISTENED FOR, had been published the previous year. Then began the long publishing hiatus that only a strengthened, less diffident Francis could have endured. Things besides government service had provided other moults: his home-leaving, meeting new, strong people he could learn from, then building his own home, as well as the daily toughening afforded by his perseverance and commitment. If he was going to have to suffer—and he was—he was better prepared now than he'd ever been. Ironically, he chose this very time to stop giving violin lessons, thus putting the burden of his livelihood entirely upon his writing.

During this sixteen-year period, his writing demonstrated a variety of phases, shifting back and forth between prose and poetry, depending upon how discouraged he became with one or the other. But more and more he turned to prose, laboring over a number of projects that never saw print, including an especially time-consuming and frustrating non-fiction book, TRAVELLING IN CONCORD. Even the success of his novella, WE FLY AWAY, in 1948 had little restorative effect on

Introduction

the poet in him. He missed poetry badly and yet too often when he wrote it, it did not succeed, either for him or for the editors and publishers to whom he submitted it.

Then something happened. As he described it to me, he began feeling a need in his life for "warmth, light, movement and excitement" and he started to develop these in his poetry. He experimented, became bolder. In June, 1952, after a protracted period of prose writing, finally coming to terms with himself as a poet, he wrote in a letter to me:

> You ask about my writing. I have made a return—a slow, thoughtful return, to poetry. I am in the midst of a new poem now. I have been too casual about my poetry in the past, though a certain casualness is good as an ingredient. I want to pour into my poetry everything I have to give. If I fail to make the market with it, it will not be so hard as failing with something less important. For, failure or not, I shall have the poetry. Poetry is what excites me most deeply. It is on my poetry that my tiny reputation rests. At last I seem to have recognized that, for better or for worse, I am a poet. What poems will come out of this fuller realization, we shall see. . . ."

Rereading this after 33 years and aided by history, I am struck more deeply now by the strength of his resolve. I also recall that the man who wrote this passionate statement about poetry would later say that he disliked it. Of course, as he explained in his autobiography, by poetry he meant the work of some of his contemporaries, certainly not the art itself or the making of poetry, which he continues to this day. But his public denunciation is important for what it reveals about the man as a poet.

When he wrote it, Francis was looking back on a lifetime that

Introduction

included many days made painful by his decision to become and remain a poet. It was not only the rejection slips, the slow progress, the sometimes cruel criticism. It was also his not having felt himself part of the world of poetry for so many years, the feeling that he didn't deserve recognition. If, as he later told me, this feeling of unworthiness helped to ease his disappointments, still it would be trying to make Francis more remarkable than he is to suggest that he passed through his years of neglect without a trace of resentment. Combine this with the fact that he brings a dutifulness to his honesty, and his denunciation is as understandable as it is tame: he found much—though certainly not all—of the poetry written by his contemporaries to be boring or baffling or both, and at the age of 70 he felt both an opportunity and an obligation to declare that he did.

But in 1952 at the age of 51 he was concentrating more than ever on making his own poetry rather than being unhappy with the work of others. He resumed writing boldly and with liveliness and soon found his work appearing in magazines formerly closed to him, *The New Yorker* and *The Saturday Review*. Beginning in 1960 with his book, THE ORB WEAVER, he would go on to publish four new books of poems. Although he would write in protest against the pollution of America's environment and against U.S. involvement in Viet Nam—and participate in weekly vigils on the Amherst Common protesting the war—he never tried to be fashionable and would not become widely popular. Nonetheless, in 1984, after a career lit by relatively few prizes, he received the Academy of American Poets' award for distinguished poetic achievement.

Once when Francis discussed this Journal with me, he said he had continued it until he decided he was "saying enough about myself in other ways." In retrospect, that speaks a great

Introduction

deal louder about his state of mind in 1954 when he finally closed the Journal, than even he may have known.

After all, there he was, writing better, more determined than ever, meeting and befriending people, beginning to teach poetry workshops and read his poetry around the country, truly on the eve of many fine poems that, in their uniquely quiet way, would enlighten and surprise as nothing he had ever done before.

Richard Gillman

TRAVELLING IN AMHERST

February 3, 1931

Sometimes it seems as easy to begin a new life as it is to step through a door into the next room. At other times it is more like breaking through a doorless wall. Let us change rooms while the doors are open.

February 11

I have two windows in my study. One is a high window that gets the sun. The other is a lower window that keeps, in winter, exclusively in the shade. Last week I watched and treasured the icicles forming outside my sunny window, speculated on their length and length of life, tried them by sunshine, moonlight, and snow-whiteness, and when at last the sun became too bright and they fell, regretted their ruin. Now I perceive that the weather that was too warm for the South icicles was just right for those by the North window. Indeed, they are longer and fatter and more rakish than the others.

Sometimes I muse, What good is this leisure and liberty and Waldenesque life? Where are they getting me? And then something happens to prove to me that in the long run I am wise. This morning as I lay in bed the conception of a poem came to me. Without interfering with mine or anyone else's program, I lay quietly for the few minutes required for the poem to catch fire. Then after breakfast, I did not drive myself to an eight-hour job, smoldering with impatience and rebellion, but I sat down in my study and burned cosily the whole morning. At dinner time the verses were done. After dinner I spent a couple of hours in altering two or three words elaborately. Now the poem is done again. And now I am beginning to see the deep virtues in leisure and liberty. How could I have foreseen that it would be precisely on this morning that I would write the best poem of my life thus far?

February 28

. . . Now and then during my walk I would stop and stand still for a few moments. At such times I could hear

1931

the trickling of running water, and the occasional crumple of a bit of snow collapsing of its own weight under the heat. . . . no trickle of water sounds more joyful and thrilling than that that runs from a snow bank on a warmish afternoon. At the crest of the hill under my "lookout pine" I found the ground not only bare but dry and warm and sunny. Though I was wearing only a couple of light sweaters and no cap, I lay down and stretched out and invited the sunshine almost as if it had been May or June. I love this world of sky and ground and hill and growing things so dearly that I am a little troubled by my externality. I feel an urge to pierce through the familiar aspect, the habitual appearance, and to seize essences.

April 24

I was holding a large bouquet of shad blossoms before my eyes to shade them from the low sun on my way home. Suddenly between the sun and me floated a big bird, white, fluffy, soundless, like an enormous thistledown drifting across the road and disappearing into the wood. Was it a white owl?

June 24

Happening last evening to look out the window toward the church where the Sunday School was having a supper, I saw Dick Schoonmaker standing outside in a corner putting his handkerchief to his nose as if he had a nosebleed. I went across the road to ask him if he didn't

1931

want to come into the house and lie down. At first he said he guessed not, his nosebleed being about over.

"Did you come over just to ask me that, Bob?"

"Yes," I said.

"Well then, I guess I'll go," he said looking up at me appreciatively and putting his arm in mine.

July 3

Thoreau went to Walden to escape the village, but not to escape himself. He went to find himself, to find life. Whenever a man cuts himself off partially or wholly from his fellows and simplifies his mode of life in order to have more of life and to become better acquainted with himself, he is following Thoreau. But living on a mountain or in a desert or in a treetop may be semi-suicide, a giving up, a closing one's eyes and stopping one's ears, a mere stunt. When Stevenson called Thoreau's experiment a retreat, he missed the point entirely.

July 5

A number of these weeds make good greens. Mr. Dwight says if he had his way he wouldn't plant spinach and Swiss chard in his garden, but pick his greens from the wild garden of dandelion, cowslip, pussly (purslane), ragweed (lamb's quarters) and milkweed. He says they taste better and are better for you.

Is it possible that these weeds that I fight so assiduously

1931

are really my friends? Is it possible that cooperation will bring me riches that extermination never dreamed of?

July 9

When a poem and I embrace, I have a peculiar impulse to pray, "Don't let me die, dear God, till this is over." The writing of poetry suddenly makes my life of high value to me.

July 22

How comprehensive and various is the realm of unbelief! Here are some of the classes:
1. What I distinctly disbelieve.
2. What I regard as more improbable than probable.
3. What I think is, at present at least, unknowable.
4. What is knowable but on which I have suspended judgment.
5. What I accept as true only in a certain sense, not in the generally accepted sense.
6. What I am too little interested in to hold any opinion about.
7. What I am merely ignorant of.

Why do I enjoy plentiful solitude? Because it brings me greater harmony with myself and my environment than does any sort of social life, and because in solitude my

1931

mind is more active on a contemplative and creative plane than when I am with people. The stimulation that some people get only in society I get only in solitude. I have a self-fertilizing mind.

October 13

In the morning writing is a marathon. In the afternoon it is a hike. And in the evening it is a climb.

October 16

I came near disgracing myself in church this morning. I could not keep my face sober to save my soul. Father being away at a convention in Portland, Mr. Pierpont was the preacher. But that was not the joke. The joke was the color on the platform. Dick and I had carried over leaves, flowers, and plants until the front of the church was swimming with golden light—maple leaves scarlet and yellow, gold-edged coleus, gold and burnt-orange calendulas, green ferns and rich-leaved begonia. And hideous as are the stained glass windows, they shed just the right light to bring out the mellowness of the colors. The joke came when I stepped into church an hour later and found Mr. Pierpont's gaunt white and black wreathed and garlanded with this autumnal riot. There it was and nobody daring to do a thing about it. People who had come to church out of duty forgot duty and enjoyed themselves. We all looked as if we were listening to the sermon while we drank in great draughts of color. Even the sleepers

1931

weren't quite so sleeping. And so a smile kept playing over my face—right through the sermon.

October 26

Picture several tall, golden maple trees and the ground beneath covered a foot deep with leaves. Picture five urchins scampering and elbowing about in the crisp billows, silent and busy as little squirrels, scooping the golden stuff into huge sacks. Fifteen bulging sackfuls from one tree! What are you going to do with them? Bedding for winter.

I have done no useful work today. But I have played the violin before a large audience, acquired a new pupil, read from *Lavengro,* walked out at sunset, and written three poems.

December 1

A bill for money owed me lies on my desk. I cannot send it now because it requires a two-cent stamp and I have exactly one cent in my cash box.

December 8

Late in the afternoon I drove up to Mrs. Hopkins' where I sat in her pewter kitchen or before the Franklin stove in her study and listened to her tell me what she thought

1931

of me. Her words were unminced, incisive, stimulating. My personality has "slipped a cog somewhere." I lack the "fear-inspiring element." I am too inexperienced to write with authority, my work being amateur. My reactions? Humiliation, stimulation, adjustment, disproof.

December 10

What a different person a drop of a few degrees in temperature makes of me! In summer I am a Latin; in winter, a Teuton.

If I had never seen paintings and etchings of shadows on snow I think I should not have felt the beauty of foot prints on my walk tonight.

December 12

I have at last finished Proust's novel in eight sub-novels (God knows how many volumes). Proust himself died before his last instalment was quite finished. His principal translator also died before he had translated the last book. Behold me, who have both finished it and live.

1932

February 6, 1932

Robert Frost has bought a house in Amherst. For a number of years he has lived part of the winter in Amherst, serving as ornament and ferment to Amherst College. Now Amherst is his home.

I have passed on this bit of good news to several people, but no one has evinced any enthusiasm over it. The people who know Frost take it as a matter of course. Many people not only don't know him; they scarcely know of him. I don't know him personally; but I regard his coming to Amherst as a personal bit of good fortune.

March 7

On Saturday afternoon I celebrated the fine spring weather by walking out to the Schurr farm and back. On the way out I encountered Mr. Richardson perched in an apple tree, pruning. He was still at the job when I returned. I said to him, "I've had three signs of spring today. The first was when I saw and heard two bluebirds. The second was seeing a boy run to a maple tree to take the pail before it overflowed. And the third was hearing a man singing outdoors at the top of his voice from the top of a tree." He grinned for he was the man. I had heard his singing from up in the woods.

March 13

Yesterday morning I received word that the Virginia Quarterly Review had accepted my two sonnets for pub-

1932

lication. Mr. Barr's letter was almost enthusiastic. Although I am too calloused and sodden by years of failure to get much sheer happiness from the event, I have derived considerable assurance from it. So I can write first class poetry after all. Now I can *afford* to starve.

Yesterday afternoon two cords of wood were put into our cellar. Two cords of wood, price fifteen dollars. Two sonnets, price fourteen dollars. I stood in the cellar looking at the small mountain of wood, and thinking.

March 14

March is the only month of the year when I am kept in the house by the weather. What fall rains and winter snow have failed to do early spring wind succeeds in doing. I could go out, of course. But the going would be perpetual struggle. And struggle is not what I wish in my walks. I hope, however, that I shall never dislike the wind merely because it keeps me indoors. I like the idea of the wind; I have written admiringly of it more than once; and I regard the March skyscapes as the finest of the year. But the sound of the wind, a week of wind such as we have been having, gets on my nerves a little. I am not like Ephraim: I do not feed on wind.

I have not yet met Robert Frost. But I feel his influence in anticipation.

1932

March 15

A sound mind and a sensitive emotional equipment, thirty years of living, innumerable educational advantages including two degrees, five years of apprenticeship with wide margins of leisure, several hundred rejection slips, some encouragement: all this and these are behind that acceptance the other day of two of my poems by the Virginia Quarterly Review. Does the result seem incommensurate with the antecedents? What a price for such a small achievement! And yet that achievement, more than anything else in my experience, has made me a poet to myself.

March 17

A few days ago I watched a man help a chicken to get born. And then start to help another, but give up, as not worth the bother.

Years ago I read of a highly skilled craftsman who was employed to remove excessive coatings of varnish from old paintings. He did the rubbing away with his thumb, a thumb that had grown extraordinarily sensitive to distinguish the feeling of varnish from the feeling of paint, and which had also grown, naturally, though paradoxically, callous. That callous, sensitive thumb has been to me a

1932

symbol of the well-adapted artist in his reaction to criticism—or to all life, for that matter.

April 4

It is good to see the golden bees climb into the purple crocus bells. It is also good to see the gray rats at the dump pounce on the garbage I bring there, see them scurry off with old potato skins for their children. Both are spring, both are life.

May 5

Mrs. M, Mrs. B's mother, laments the late spring. But if my memory is not too defective, every spring is later than it should be. And yet the red maples and the marsh marigolds, the crocuses and daffodils and bluets and anemones all blossom about their accustomed time each year. The sun is hot and the wind is cold, and that is about all that can be said. Many of the flowers are close enough to the ground not to feel the wind. I have also been close enough to the ground many a time this spring already to feel the sun hot on my undisguised body. It's the secret of finding spring early.

I am reading Bliss Perry's *Emerson Today,* a gentle and gentlemanly, as well as authoritative presentation of our

1932

great American. I see Emerson in it all, and hear Perry, that staunch upholder of the gentlemanly tradition. The book goes to my heart, and to my conscience. I feel as if some of the shrewd observations were put in for my particular benefit.

May 9

After reading in Phillips Russel's book, *Emerson, the Wisest American,* I sat by the window in my bedroom, thinking into the twilight. A sprig of golden currant made the air about me redolent. The peepers in the marsh made the outdoors air silvery. The new moon and the evening planet were in conjunction above the apple tree. Beneath the tree sat a white cat with a black spot on its back. In Dwights' shed a light was burning. Another light gleamed from Mr. Barton's study farther off. At such moments I grow sane and ripe. I must have more of them.

How may a secular age take over the technique of devoted living from the age of religion?

May 10

Here is the purpose and the will to achieve the purpose. Here is time. Here is the task. Gentlemen, let me make you acquainted with one another.

1932

May 12

If we have not the basis for the good life in the present age, can we not devote ourselves to the search for it?

June 30

In these rare but precious poetic moods poetry comes first in my life. I drop everything else for it. It integrates me, makes me feel immortal, absorbs me completely. At other times the philosophic mood is dominant. Then the impulse to reason, understand, clarify is uppermost. I think I can plot my life according to these two motives.

July 29

The most uninteresting thing in the world is a comprehensive view. Partial views, one-angled views are what we live on. They are what fill magazines. The man who sees all sides of a question is never a lively conversationalist. He always agrees with your partial view partly; he never agrees with it wholly.

July 30

Reading a book is almost as hard for Father as writing a book is for me.

July 31

I have just written one of my tiniest and loveliest poems, "Bronze." Now that it is all over I am interested in noting

1932

several significant things. The idea and feeling of the poem had been in my mind for at least two years. The actual composition came immediately after an afternoon nap. . . .

While writing the poem I noticed once more how extremely irritating ordinary sounds as of voices could be which at other times would not have interrupted or annoyed me in the least. The writing of poetry being my most deeply creative act, I feel toward the slightest marring of the atmosphere, the slightest hint of interference not only with my activity but with my thought and mood, as one feels during sexual orgasm. Interruption is simply intolerable.

My attitude toward writing in general is like that of a happily married man toward his wife. Writing to me is not a bright, visualized, sharply defined desire (as it is to those who wish to write but in fact do not); rather it is a need, an ingrained experience, so deep that I am not usually aware of it. Only when the need becomes acute or is thwarted do I realize that for good or ill I am doomed to be a writer. Just as I am doomed, while I live, to be an eater and a sleeper and a dreamer. Writing is not my sweetheart; it is my wife, it is part of me.

1932

Bronze

Boy over water,
Boy waiting to plunge
Into still water
Among white clouds
That will shatter
Into bright foam—
I could wish you
Forever bronze
And the blue water
Never broken.

1932

August 7

The most beautiful sight I have seen recently was the expression on Dick Schoonmaker's face the other evening as he sat in front of his little sister asking her questions. Ruth had waked from sleep early in the night and Mrs. Schoonmaker had brought her down stairs. There she sat in her nightie on the sofa in the livingroom while three of the boys sat about her watching with utter absorption. I watched her too, and also Dick as he watched her. In the dim light all blemishes of his complexion and the contour of his face were hidden and only his essential and most expressive beauty was revealed. At one moment his eyes were wide with fascinated wonder, then they would take on a dark luminousness as if he saw very deeply, and again the eyes would seem to flush in a quick realization of the sheer humor of the little mite before him. In asking a question he would purse his lips a little and speak very clearly and gently. "Ruth," he would begin with a soothing upward inflection and in such a warm, mellow, open-throated voice as I have heard in no one else. And as he waited for her answer, his lips would seem to be forming the words for her in eagerness and sympathy. I remember so well those pursed, sensitive, smiling lips, and that slight backward tilting of the head, and the eager raising of the shoulders. Sometimes he would draw back a little, holding his head a bit to this side or that like an artist criticizing a picture or a girl trimming something. Then would come a toss of the hair and a forward thrust of the face and the brightening of the eyes and the curve

1932

of the lips and the warm, mellow voice. Between times would come swift glances of suppressed mirth at me and winks and knowing grimaces. The next moment he had forgotten me utterly and was absorbed in the little sister.

August 9

Man desires fixity. Fixity in knowledge is certainty, philosophic absolutism, religious dogma. In material goods, it is possession. In a world of chance, it is safety. In a world of ever-repeating birth and death, it is immortality. But all fixity is a dream, and when man wakes from his dream he wakes into disillusion. Let us base our lives on the ceaseless flow and change of things. Rapid metabolism means health. Constant shifting of emotional attachment during childhood and adolescence means normal development. Let us not be disturbed at finding ourselves changing or our friends changing; let us rather be disturbed if we do not change.

August 22

The allegory of the tower is suggestive. When philosophy means escape, the tower is the proverbial one of ivory. When philosophy means revelation, the tower is a minaret or steeple that brings one nearer heaven and heaven's enlightenment. But for me philosophy is just an observatory that lifts one above the tree line. From such a

1933

tower one can see the whole forest and not mere individual trees. From such a tower one can find directions and plot one's course better than from the ground. And the relative sizes and relations of objects lie clear to the view. All of which is useful for life, and beautiful in a way that single leaves and individual trees are not.

September 15

My highest purpose is to help other people realize their own highest purposes. I focus my attention on the other person's best aspirations (whether active or latent), and try, in ways more subtle than obvious, to quicken and release those aspirations. I am less eager to add to the world's large stock of wisdom than I am to stimulate people to follow the wisdom they already have.

January 13, 1933

One rainy afternoon not quite eight years ago something happened to me that I have never forgotten. It was the nearest to a vision or revelation that I shall probably ever have. The idea was very simple; but the compelling force of it was something to treasure. It seems now as though this dream might begin to be realized soon, not because I have the means, but only because I have the urgent desire. The dream, of course, is simply that of a little farm house off in the backwoods somewhere, but

1933

preferably not too far from Amherst, which I may own and help repair and in which I may live and be happy.

January 24

Today I started a savings account with a ten-dollar deposit; and I met Robert Frost.

February 2

The placid friendship between Mrs. Hopkins and me has at last received a jolt. Perhaps it was inevitable. Last Saturday at her suggestion and request I took up cigarette smoking. Day before yesterday I decided to give it up. When I told her this today, she brought all her guns into play against me. I was polite, kindly, but obdurate. The more important she showed me she regarded my smoking, the more important my not smoking seemed to me. Still more important, to both of us, was the question whether or not I was to do something on her say-so. Whereas she struck blindly, so to speak, I was perfectly controlled and thus will have no apologies to make. When I left the house, I felt buoyant. It was as if an evil enchantment had been broken. I felt like singing. Nothing that has happened recently has bucked me up more than this. Having declared my independence I feel more of a man.

1933

Yesterday morning while out walking I asked myself what I really wanted. Three things, the answer was: a life, a person, and a book. The life is the life that I want to live and that I am in a small degree already living; a life of health, sunshine, outdoor activity, beautiful surroundings, leisure, friendship, and solitude. The person is the unknown person with whom I want to share this life and for whom I want to devote it. The book is the half-imagined volume that I might write out of such a life; one of those rare books that gives life itself to the reader; a book that one might stake one's own life upon.

March 12

We have no word for our collective political life. Politics denotes the activity of politicians, not of citizens; and has fallen to the status of chicanery. Civics is an academic subject taught to high school pupils. Patriotism is a waving of flags. Does the absence of a word imply the absence of the reality?

March 31

On my walk to Hadley this morning I was reminded of what someone told me an old man in Amherst used to say this time of year. "We won't have warmer weather until the snow has melted from the Williamsburg hills, and the snow won't melt from the Williamsburg hills until we have warmer weather."

1933

Something in me says, "You should read this book word for word from cover to cover." Something else contradicts with: "You know from experience that you have almost never found a book that was worth reading entire. Don't waste your time over this one whatever its pretensions. Bite into it the way the Children of Israel bolted their Pentacostal meal, or the way a traveling salesman consumes a piece of apple pie at the stand-up counter of the Bingville Junction Depot where the train waits five minutes to take in water."

April 3

This afternoon Mrs. Shumway and I played the entire César Franck Sonata before the Women's Club at Masonic Hall. On the whole it went well.

My acquaintance with this sonata dates from my college days; in the music appreciation course I took someone played the sonata, and it was treated in our text book. The year I was in Syria I bought the music. Dave Hall and I dipped into it here and there, but neither of us could begin to play it. The next year Miss Sproule and I worked at it in the old house in Lynn, finding it decidedly beyond us. I think Ted Ward and I must have taken a whack or two at it during those memorable afternoons in Pelham. Miss Kidder and I got so far as to attempt one

1933

or two movements in public somewhere long ago. And now for well over a year Mrs. Shumway and I have been really working on this beautiful music. Last April we essayed the first and fourth movements before the Parent-Teacher Association at the Munson Building. Now today we play the whole thing, I without notes, of course. And it went not too badly. At least I didn't feel like hanging my head afterwards.

I go thus into detail because this little story illustrates the process of gathering up the past and projecting it into the future, a process that I am learning, a conscious weaving of life into patterns. In one sense we have finished the sonata; in another sense we shall probably never finish it.

April 7

My determining reason for going to the Hopkins' this summer is economic. In return for garden work and driving I have rooms where I can make my headquarters, get my meals cheaply, reach my pupils easily, and be quiet for writing. Until the middle of September—that is through the slack season—I am spared all financial worry.

April 17

What shall I hang on my walls (when I have walls of my own)?

1933

May 3

After days of warm sunshine a heavy rain fell this afternoon, and now the air is full of delicious and unaccountable fragrances. At my elbow is a bouquet of delicious arbutus. On the Strong House grounds is another, larger bouquet—a cherry in bloom. The forsythias are golden. At the library my little herb garden now contains tansy, bee balm, costmary, two thymes, lavender, southernwood, winter savory, sage, lavender-cotton, rosemary, sweet marjoram, pennyroyal, mint, and burnet. I spent several hours yesterday in putting the remnants of my old herb garden in South Amherst in more presentable order. Here at my room five of nine plantings of seeds are coming up. And from England today came more seeds—elecampane, sweet Cicely, musk, woodruff, and camomile.

June 8

Mrs. Hopkins has helped me, but not altogether in the ways that she probably thinks she has. She has helped me by rubbing my fur the wrong way and thus sharpening my awareness of myself. What I was before I have become more explicitly through her judgments, her efforts, and her example. Thus she has unwittingly confirmed my inclination away from the fictional, the dramatic, and the accumulating; and toward the factual, the philosophic, and the simple. Her sweeping dicta, e.g., that I have not the "oriental love of color" or a sense of line and form, and that I lack energy, have prodded me to examine my actual condition, and perhaps to amend it a little.

Mrs. Hopkins has also helped me by forcing me, without her knowing it, into certain habits of work and policies of social life in pure self-defence. To live at all with her I had to live a certain way. Now I find those habits and policies valuable anywhere.

For the home that she has provided me for two years I have paid her in work in full. For introducing me to Robert Frost and for securing a free hospital operation for me, I suppose I can never repay her.

But whatever I have learned from her directly or indirectly, through her intent or in spite of it, has been learned. I have learned my lessons and have graduated.

June 22

The poet is a spider, forever spinning. The novelist is a caterpillar, eating, eating great slices of life. But the poet spins his poetry out of himself, out of next to nothing.

June 29

Trees cannot be really seen by daylight. It needs the hour between dusk and night. Then you can see their patience, their rootedness. You see how two trees live side by side together. How families of trees keep one another company. You see the solitary, self-sufficient trees. And there is the strange intercourse of wind with trees whose sound one so easily fails to hear by day.

1933

October 2

I have been pouring over the grim pictures in the recent photographic history of the war by Stallings. From a human point of view the war was as big a thing as ever happened, and as terrible. A preacher whom I heard yesterday said that it ended the 19th Century. Doubtless it did, together with some million human lives. It did not end, however, and it did not begin the problems that interest me most deeply. These are the problems that have interested men since they began to think and will interest them until they stop thinking. When the problems of war and of the machine age are all solved, these other problems will remain.

October 3

From my study on the top floor of the Jones Library I look out on a picture in green, blue, and gray. The fluttering foliage of a big cottonwood tree nearly fills the frame with the blue of sky showing through the branches. The gray is a beautiful stone chimney and bit of roof on an L of the building. I see scarcely any ground except when I rise up a little. Then I can see the granite stones and the varied greens of the herb garden. Through the tree is one spot of deeper blue, a segment of a distant hill.

This is the picture that I look at morning after morning as I glance aside from my desk in the room which I have devoted to poetry. What effect have this tree, this sky, this hill, and this stone had on what I have thought and written here?

October 20

About a month ago when I was on the crest of my summer's creative work I sent twenty-five poems to nine magazines. They have all come back except one, and none received comment. But this is an old, old story. Don't let me try to squeeze one drop of self-pity from this unremarkable event.

October 25

Rain and wind and cold weather at last. The big cottonwood tree near my window at the library is much thinned of its leaves. Beneath it are little crimson-pink bushes. The ivy on the gray walls is also red. I can see that my basil plants have succumbed, although the other greens of the herb garden are unchanged. Here in my study it is warm and quiet and familiar. I am thankful.

I see all the evil of the world as a black tapestry against which and within which man is to weave the golden threads of his life. He can never blot out the black. He can only weave a more and more beautiful pattern. If he could blot out the black, where would his pattern be?

1933

Not quite, not quite have I yet learned that I am a poet. It is a fact that I must learn over many times before I have truly grasped it. It is so much to believe. When people call me a poet, I turn the remark aside like a bad joke, instead of suffering the designation.

October 26

Valéry regards form in poetry as a self-imposed difficulty of the poet, a rule of the game. To him it makes little difference how irrational the form may be just so it involves difficulty agreed upon.

I too champion form, but I want form to be the perfect expression of the content. I want form to fit feeling as skin fits flesh.

October 27

I think it is Valéry who says that the experience behind the poem is less than the experience of the poem. I have heard the same thought elsewhere. Certainly it is true of me. To judge from my poetry my life has been richer in emotion and deeper in thought than it really has been. Art is more a fulfillment of experience than a mere record of it.

Not until the other day, I think, have I fully realized the value to me of reading or speaking aloud my poems.

1933

Nothing else makes me so aware of my power as a human being and develops that power. I can actually feel myself growing. Nothing else, also, makes me so confident of my poetry than recreating it in this way.

I am reading Niehardt's *Poetic Values*. It is a plea for the recognition of "expanded states of consciousness" in the creation and enjoyment of poetry and the other arts. Having just read Valéry's *Variety* which, among other things, is a defense of the conscious mind, I am interested to follow it with this defense of various dream states. I am a little confused by what I think is the author's confusion. He contrasts the prosaic, narrow, sense-bound character of the ordinary focus of attention with the wider awareness in subliminal or dream states. But are there not vast upward ranges in the conscious state? May not a refinement of consciousness produce exalted poetry at times, and may not a dream (of any sort) sometimes lead to inferior poetry?

"The true value of such inspirations does not depend on the obscurity of their origin, or on the supposed depth from which we are simple enough to believe that they came, or on the exquisite surprise they cause to ourselves;

1933

it depends rather on their meeting our needs, and, in the final analysis, on the conscious use we make of them—in other words, on the collaboration of the whole man."
Valéry in *An Introduction to the Method of Leonardo Da Vinci*

November 21

Last Friday I spent nearly two hours with Robert Frost at his home. . . . Picture the poet lolling in a big chair, his hair getting more and more rumpled, and his words billowing on with the freedom and abundance of the ocean. . . . He began on the subjects of stimulants by saying he distrusted anything but outdoor health. . . . But fatigue can be a drug as well as can hard drink. Mr. Frost has a notion he could go through a volume of poetry and pick out the poems written in the morning and those written at night and under fatigue. This idea brought up the problem of what part of one's mind should be used in writing poetry. Frost doesn't like the word "subconscious." He simply says that the creation of a poem begins in a state. In a good poet this state is highly specialized. Only a particular kind of poem will satisfy it. Some poets write verse from a generalized state like the craving for sweet; anything sweet and sugary satisfies them. The true poet can be satisfied with nothing but an expression of his particular mood which may be very subtle and impossible to analyze. If he allows himself to get switched off, he may achieve a kind of specious success with the poem, but in his heart he will know it is a failure.

1933

Emily Dickinson is a poet whose "state" never gets sidetracked. Since she wrote without thought of publication and was not under the necessity of revamping and polishing, it was easy for her to go right to the point and say precisely what she thought and felt. Her technical irregularities give her poems strength as if she were saying, "Look out, Rhyme and Meter, here I come." Frost likes this wilfulness, this unmanageability of the thought by the form, but he thinks it was a little too easily arrived at by Emily Dickinson in whom it is sometimes indistinguishable from carelessness. In other words, she gave up the technical struggle too easily.

November 24

Imagination like a great tree rooted in the subconscious and thrusting its branches into the sky of sheer fantasy. I feel now that I can create gorgeous imaginative poetry—things that never were on land and sea. I have not done anything of this sort, not so much because I was not able to as because my attention had not been sufficiently called to the possibility. It seems to me that such poetry would be twice as much fun to write as the sort I have written, fun as that has been. . . . I should like to let myself go and live richly and fabulously in my poetry. Has it been a trace still of the New England conscience that has held me from this? Have I wanted to be so true to the facts, so moral, so philosophical, so grown-up that I could not let myself go? Well, it may turn out that I can combine all these things.

1933

Last night I went down to the football field under the moon. As I went down through the tennis courts, terrace after terrace, I reminded myself in my mysterious solitude of some Aztec priest descending a sacrificial mound. What would another person have thought if he could have seen me pacing back and forth across the great level field and sometimes breaking into a run? Something about the flat surface looking off to hills and valley, the bright moon, the sounds coming in clear from a distance took me back to Beirut where on so many nights I walked across the campus by moonlight and felt the buildings, the mountains, and the sea.

November 27

Last Saturday afternoon I went down to South Amherst to spend a while with my parents and have supper with them. We gathered about the open fire in the upstairs study. Then it was I did a thing for which I have not ceased to give thanks. I repeated some of my poems for them. A week before I doubt if I would have thought of such a thing.

1934

May 2, 1934

The red maples and the rock maples have divided the spring between them. Right up to the end of April the red blossoms of the former were the most conspicuous color among trees. Now the pale green gold of the rock maple blossoms holds precedence. I celebrated May Day by taking the sun and by planting herb seeds. I also went over to Mt. Holyoke last night to hear Lawrence Binyon talk on Blake, but this did not prove to be a particularly spring-like occasion. Oh, these lectures! One is forced to ask the embarrassing question: Does this lecture offer more than what could be gained with less time and effort and no expense from a book? Lectures are generally an academic anachronism, dating from the centuries before the spread of printing, and lingering on under pleasant campus elms like caps and gowns.

May 3

A quiet rain. Etherealized water. There is no more soothing sound than this soft rustle and trickle and subdued gurgling. The tree trunks are black and the new, limp-hanging blossoms are pale gold to the half-closed eye.

Samson's riddle: out of the strong came forth sweetness.

1934

Religion: hide and seek.

May 10

Thoreau is right. If one has the good fortune to be poor, he should let nothing interfere with his full enjoyment of his poverty.

Frost is right. If the young writer is unpublished, he should cultivate the full and sheer and unadulterated joy of writing.

May 21

Yesterday afternoon I had a rare experience. I had gone to Butter Hill alone, climbed to the top in leisurely fashion, and was thinking of going down the other side in order to look up a family on the Gulf Road. I had heard that Allen Ross, a boy who worked for Mr. Atkins a couple of years ago, lived there and had a little printing establishment on his own. I was curious to see it. Allen was not home, but his father, a sturdy, sunburned, spirited man, proudly showed me the printing plant and told me about his son, or rather, his eldest son, for there are nine children in the family. There in an attic room of the old farm house were the small presses, the trays of type, and the various odds and ends that the boy had been able to afford. When I saw samples of his printing, I was really surprised, and the venture seemed praiseworthy as well as picturesque. Allen is enterprising in getting work, and shows both pride and skill in turning out a good job. He has a car and gets about a good deal. The printer in Belchertown is glad to call him in when he needs extra help.

I don't know when a man has made a better impression on me than the father. The things he said were so unaffected and to the point. He told me that a week's groceries yesterday cost him just $20; that he was glad to spend his money in food for his family rather than in doctor's bills; that not one of his nine children had ever had a doctor except when five of them had their tonsils out at the same time. Coming out of the house, he pointed to his apple trees still in bloom and said, "I'm as much interested in those as Allen is in his printing." . . .

Well, the little visit did me lots of good. I felt I was ready to go back to my own work.

May 27

Yesterday afternoon I called on the elder Mr. Whicher and was shown his garden. But though the garden seemed delightful to me, and would have been delightful even had it not been so finished and well-cared-for, to Mr. Whicher it was one long reminder of regret. There were not nearly as many plants in bloom, he told me, as there ought to be at this time and as there used to be in other years. The winter had killed so many plants. I pointed to some pink lady slippers under a pine tree, only to be as-

1934

sured that they were smaller this year even though they had come up. Ferns were a great source of joy to him, he confessed, but he did not like the "interruption" of the interrupted fern. Another plant he had in the garden because his wife liked it, although he did not. He was sorry his columbines were not the long-spurred variety which he thought much handsomer than those he had. Complimented on his thriving patch of tansy, he lamented that it had to be slashed to be kept in bounds. To judge by his words, the garden was a source of exquisite pain to the old man. All the more pathos, then, in his exclamation that he was so thankful to be living one more spring to enjoy it.

June 11

A week ago Friday I had a session with Frost. Although I was suffering from a severe cold (fool I was to go in such a condition), a cold that laid me up for a week and from which I have not yet entirely recovered,—I think I have never been more moved by Mr. Frost's conversation than I was that morning. Certainly he has never been more luminous and kindly.

I had told him of the series of disappointments I had just had regarding editors and publishers, and much that he said was by way of consolation, although he explicitly denied that he was doing that. "Of course," he said, "you can always get better. There is always room for improvement in any poet; and if publication is deferred, you have a chance to be more selective." He said he was really glad

1934

that he had had to wait for publication, and he admitted that he was not ashamed of the way he had taken the waiting. He went on living and writing and did not regard his failure with the publishers too seriously. But there did come a time when he gathered his forces together in an effort to force the publishers to recognize; he places that turning-point in his morale at the time when he gave up farming for a return to teaching.

November 1

He (James Stephens) is a little Irishman, one of the Little Men, with a wan face that goes up to a head bald in the center and bushy black on either side, a twist to the body, and a limp to the walk. But he has the Irish magic. (Last night was Hallowe'en.) Never have I heard anyone talk more provocatively about poetry than he.

For convenience he divided poetry into three sorts and gave illustrations of each: talking, balancing, and singing. He made a memorable distinction between emotion and passion: the great poets have the latter and the lesser poets the former. A poet's failure to write great poetry he attributed to lack of will (the total force of the personality) rather than to lack of intelligence, emotion, imagination, or industry. Poetry can dispense with meaning and emotion, but to be great it must have passion. Stephens commented on the fact that almost no poetry has been written about air or fire or water or other common things such as birds. Shelley's "Sky-Lark" is unpardonable, and to think Shelley did it! The way to write about a bird or

1935

a cat—and he gave us his about the cat—is to tell how the animal makes us feel, to be birdlike or catlike. An easier thing, this, for little Stephens than for some of the rest of us. . . . The sallies of wit were endless. Abracadabra was once a convenient word to hide behind. Now we have psychology and the psychological approach. Frost being in the audience, Stephens expressed the hope that the American poet would properly go to sleep in due time. Then, a little later, he ranked Frost as second only to Emerson in American poetry, with Vachel Lindsay (at his best) third. There was a fourth, he added, but he had forgotten his name. He has a theory that the country richest in money is also richest in literature, and sees both kinds of wealth passing from England to America, in much the way that music passes from Germany to Russia, and criticism and military skill are going from France to Italy.

January 10, 1935

As a child in school Gertrude Stein's chief passion was for diagramming sentences. She is still passionate about such things, still a child.

January 23

How clearly I know what I want. Would I know so clearly if I had what I want?

1935

January 26

"I am the door." "I am the way." "I am the good shepherd." If metaphor is the heart of poetry, as Frost maintains, where is poetry to compare with this? The true, the inevitable, the fateful word. And the word is made flesh. Here is poetry that is lived as well as spoken.

In poetry distrust ornament. It is the first to wear out.

February 12

Once he was the man whose head was on the penny. A head never to be confused with that of any other man. But hasn't many a boy wondered inarticulately why he looked so gaunt, why he had to look so gaunt? I was thirty-two years old before I saw the meaning and value in those deep lines of the face. Now Lincoln becomes for me a creation myth—his body the land that made him, his bones the rocks, his blood the rivers, his dreams the clouds.

February 17

A life-subject. While still a youth Havelock Ellis determined to devote his life to the study of the psychology of sex. Now that Ellis is an old man, how complete and monumental has been that devotion.

If I too live till old age, will I have such a single and embracing loyalty to look back upon? One subject, one complex problem has haunted me more than any other

1935

these years that I have tried to write: the need and possibility of a new spiritual synthesis to take the place of the religions. I persist in thinking on this subject: I persist in writing on it. I keep coming back to it. Why is this not *my* devotion? I can think of no more important one.

March 9

I bought a pair of shoes today. There is a sober satisfaction about buying shoes that I do not feel in buying other clothing. However much I might need a new suit or a new shirt, I could still be comfortable and protected in the old ones. Not so with shoes. When I need them I need them. They are foundation, nothing fancy. Mine cost $1.69. They will give me at least half a year's hard wear.

March 10

I have been playing a game of solitaire. My cards were not all cards. Some were various-colored slips of paper or folders. All were printed with polite expressions of regret. First I sorted them, putting all of a kind together, then I counted the number in each pile. From The Atlantic Monthly there were 43, enough for a book if they had been bound. Harper's came next, 30; Scribner's, 20; Poetry, 17 (on all 17 was the same Chicago telephone number); Forum, 15; Christian Century, 14; Nation, 11; and Bookman and Century, 10 each. These were the biggest piles. Altogether there were 130 different sources of the pieces of paper. The number of pieces was 462. If you

1935

want a bigger total than that, add 179 "personal rejections." Then you will have the staggering figure: 641. Was any man ever more rejected? Am I a fool or a hero?

I began this collection about ten years ago, partly on principle, for the sake of records; then for the joke of it. I planned to burn them all upon my first considerable success. But ten years is long enough to keep a joke up one's sleeve. I had my bonfire tonight—without the success. I burned all 462 except a small pile of the neater cards which I shall use for memorandum and correspondence. The 461 minus blazed beautifully in the wind against the black, and they kept blazing a surprisingly long time. Some of the Atlantic bunch were the last to blacken. I thought they would never disappear. I stood and waited and warmed my hands.

May 2

The choosing becomes more and more urgent. At college we enjoyed the vague supposition that we could have everything. College, indeed, seems to be an institution for inculcating this very notion. If you take A this year you can take B or C next year. And every day is long enough for what you want to do—from studying to going to the movies. There is no course in choosing, no course in learning to go without.

1935

The fascination of old people is their expressiveness. All that they have been in their lives is in their faces and in their forms. Nothing is hidden.

May 22

Writing poetry is like playing the harp: it often takes as long to get in tune as it does to play.

A poetic diction is to poetry what costume is to clothing: we do not live in it.

June 6

Frost says that he likes to have discernible lumps in his poems—passages that have as much disconnectedness with the rest of the poem as they have connectedness—pieces of experience that still show their individual origin. How like the New England landscape. It is all rock underneath, but here and there the rock crops out—boulders.

Frost distrusts long poems. A poem should be written from impulse, and impulses don't last very long. The best that a long poem can be, he says, is a series of impulses, of short poems. But I could tell Frost a thing or two. I could tell him that short poems are love affairs, and a

1935

long poem is a marriage. Is a happy marriage merely a series of affairs?

June 8

The poems that I myself have rejected fill a volume larger than my volume of poems still in good standing, which I call *Men in the Landscape*. I counted the others today—seventy-four. Seventy-four poems that I once was proud of and have now rejected. These rejected poems include two that were published two years ago in the *Virginia Quarterly Review* and reprinted in the *Literary Digest;* five others published elsewhere, of one of which Benjamin Musser said it was "heartbreakingly lovely"; two that John Theobald liked best of all my work; still two others of which Aunt Harriet said, *"That*'s good," and "Now I know you are a poet"; another that drew iron praise from the *Yale Review*, and another that received a good word from the *Forum;* and finally four that were commended in whole or in part by Mr. Frost. I want to say that I can reject my own poems as well as the editors can; I can reject the very poems they accept and pay for and print.

One day a couple of weeks ago I returned to my room from the library rejoicing in a new poem written that morning. After dinner I thought I would copy it on the typewriter and make perhaps a few slight revisions. My revisions became new versions one after another until I

1935

had to give up. Some days later I started another poem, short, simple, unrhymed like the other. Its tenth version I accepted. Then I turned to the former poem and made its eleventh version which has stood thus far. For the fun of it I kept all the papers and have just counted my tries. These two are "fluid" poems. Water is hard to handle. It can't be built up neatly in lines and stanzas.

June 10

It has just occurred to me that what Frost wants a poem to be in form is like the human form—all parts organically related and proportioned, but with the parts still distinct. Not the smooth sphere in which all points on the surface are equidistant from the center, but the human body in which some parts are farther than others from the heart.

September 15

Dave asked me, "Aren't you making a mistake in persisting in this obscure, heroic kind of life?"

Hildegard asked me, "Won't it be rather difficult say twenty years from now?"

My answer is this. Every kind of life costs something. The price I pay is different from the price others pay because my life itself is different. I cannot escape payment, but I can make my life worth payment.

1935

November 10

This has been the first Sunday within a month that I have not started out at noontime with my lunch in a paper bag. Each time I have gone the same way and eaten at the same place. The way leads down the short cut to Lincoln Avenue and Sunset Avenue and along the latter till a little roadway takes one out to the field. I cross one field, climb through a fence, over another fence, diagonally across a second field, over a third fence, and along it till I come to the brook. There where pasture meets wood, the brook bends twice. In this open yet secluded place on the grassy bank I have eaten three Sunday dinners from a paper bag. The first time I ate there bluebirds were flying from tree to tree, and leaves were fluttering down to the water and drifting around one bend and then another bend out of sight. The witch-hazel blossoms here a golden mist in the sunlight. The next week the witch-hazel blossoms had shriveled, but the sunlight was still golden. And the next week. Today the sun was hidden, and I did not go.

December 4

A sudden new idea as I am walking along the street can make me take short careful steps like a person carrying something easily spilled.

1936

February 18, 1936

I am rich in mornings. I am rich in the morning. Morning after morning, month after month, year after year I go to the Jones Library for two to three hours of uninterrupted creative work. During those morning hours I desire nothing that I do not have. They are my prize possessions . . . And so the poems get written and the books get written. And so I live with myself. Who else is there in all my acquaintance who has such morning wealth?

April 15

Last Friday, Good Friday, I had word from Macmillan that they would publish my book of poems, STAND WITH ME HERE. The date will probably be sometime in the fall. Thus I shall celebrate the tenth anniversary of my coming to Amherst.

Between now and then are two other days worth mentioning. On June 8th Father will be seventy; and on August 12th I shall be thirty-five.

April 19

Gertrude Stein's *Narration,* which I have been reading, is delightful nonsense. When I say nonsense, I do not mean that it has no sense. Nonsense would not be entertaining or funny if it had no sense to it. It would not be nonsense. For nonsense one must have the tension between a passionate or pseudo-passionate meaning and misbehav-

1936

ing words. The funniest clown is he whose serious intent shows pathetically through his clowning, as in Chaplin. Gertrude Stein is in the class with Shakespeare's fools: all of them manage to get a lot of truth into their nonsense. Technically she has two tricks: to repeat a word as often and in as many combinations as possible; and to leave out most of the punctuation marks. We have her word for it that both these tricks date from her grammar school days.

1936

    I'll tell you a story
       About Jack M'Norry.
    And now my story's begun.

    I'll tell you another
       About Jack and his brother.
    And now my story is done.
                        nursery rhyme

1936

"As I say I have been very bothered about everything and I will tell about something else."

Gertrude Stein

June 9

Yesterday the Macmillan Fall List arrived. Five books of poetry are listed: a new volume by Masefield, selected poems of Vachel Lindsay, collected poems of somebody else, and among the five a certain new poet, Robert Francis.

Last summer I thought of giving up my writing and going into social work. This summer I am a Macmillan poet.

This growing need to order and collect the years, to measure one year by another, to think from summer to summer, to say these five years or these ten years, to trace complicated patterns of return—what is this in my living but the thing called form in poetry?

A time comes when the need is no longer education or stimulation or criticism or encouragement or even expe-

1937

rience, but a small room where one can think and write in quietness.

Mention of solitude makes two sorts of people jealous: those that want it but can't have it, and those that might have it but don't want it.

June 22

If solitude merely made me happy, I might hesitate to indulge it. But since it also makes me productive, I feel justified in saying no to a few picnics.

November 8

No other book do I come back to so often, no other book so unfailingly recalls me to myself as *The Heart of Emerson's Journal*. Emerson is my master.

March 16, 1937

Yesterday I did not pay an income tax or even file returns. My income for 1936 was $817. Thus my monthly average was $68 and my weekly average was $15.72.

1937

July 12

Here begins another chapter. I have been living in my new old house in Cushman since July 2. Since early spring I have been looking for a house to live in. And since a certain day in February 1925 I have definitely wanted a house to live in. The five previous places I have lived since leaving the paternal roof in the fall of 1932 have all been steps toward this. Now I am here and I like it.

July 13

I dispute possession of this house with the ghost of an old woman who has lived here I don't know how many years. She is not dead yet, but she is ninety-seven years old and that is old enough to have a ghost. She is everywhere here; but bit by bit I am getting rid of her. I am also disputing possession with innumerable animals, mostly insects. There are also some birds, a chipmunk, some mice that I have not seen, and a skunk that died in the cellar months ago.

July 28

Today I finished my long narrative poem, *Valhalla*, on which I have been working for nearly three years. Whatever becomes of the poem, I am sure that I am a better educated man, and perhaps a wiser one, than when I started it. This poem was written in the Hopkins' house,

1938

at the Jones Library, at Mrs. Boynton's, at Mrs. Newkirk's, at my parents', and lastly, here in Cushman.

February 25, 1938

After lighting my four lamps late this afternoon, I went out for a brief walk. This is a game I have played with myself more than once—turning back to see the lighted windows, then on my way back watching to see those same windows appear over the rise of the road, asking myself who lived there, thinking of the times I might have asked in earnest, finally coming home to a warm and lighted house. Good so far. Someday I may come home to more.

March 24

These four days of spring have been four spring days. Promptly on Monday the phoebes arrived. Tuesday night I heard a killdeer. Last night I heard the first peepers, and this morning the grunting frogs across the brook. Monday I changed to summer underwear. Tuesday I left off my overcoat. Wednesday I omitted my vest. Today I put on my overcoat, for we went back from late May to early April. Yesterday I took my first sun bath of the season.

1938

April 22

Two days ago, April 20, word came for which I had been waiting all winter. Macmillan has accepted my second book of poems for publication. It consists of the long narrative, "Valhalla," and a group of about thirty short poems.

April 28

Last night my bath was in the familiar tub in the kitchen. I had left the tub in the middle of the floor, the bath water still in it, and gone to bed early. Soon there was a knocking that grew in loudness and determination. It was Opportunity knocking, Opportunity incarnate in the form of a man from Northfield Seminary come to get me to substitute for Robert Hillyer Saturday evening in their lecture course. The man said he could offer me from fifty to seventy-five dollars. I said seventy-five would be satisfactory. It seems that Mr. Hillyer's doctor had ordered him to cancel all his engagements. My doctor advises me to take every seventy-five dollar engagement I can get.

July 20

It occurred to me the other day that I wanted to be but wasn't the sort of person I'd like to meet.

1939

November 1

As a precaution against its being lost I quote a letter that came yesterday from Robert Frost.

"Dear Robert: I am swept off my feet by the goodness of your poems this time. Ten or a dozen of them are my idea of perfection. A new poet swims into my ken. I can refrain from strong praise no longer. You are achieving what you live for. I shall always honor Dave for his part in your coming out. You have not only the feeling of a true lyric poet, but the variety of a man with a mind. Ever yours, Robert Frost."

January 20, 1939

When we are young we rack our brains for subjects to write about. When we are older we write about the things we can't get rid of, things that haunt us. We write about them to try to get rid of them.

March 12

On Friday I went to Boston to read for the New England Poetry Club—and wrote a poem on the train down. Saturday, yesterday, I wrote a poem on the way back. Today having sat down to copy the two on the typewriter, I wrote another. . . . Less than two weeks ago a check for

1942

$475 fell out of an unpromising envelope for me—the Shelley Memorial Award.

December 16

Eleanor Wade, a distant cousin of father's writes to him, "Where and how is your son Robert, he was such a beautiful boy when I saw him. I think I heard he was a very clever young man but that was a good while ago."

February 15, 1942

Two shadows—the loss of my father and the spread of war—have had most to do with how I felt and thought and therefore acted these past two years.

February 16

Today I registered under the Selective Service Act. I am liable to the draft.

I am a conscientious objector to combatant service. If this stand seems inconsistent, it is less inconsistent than any other I can think of. I am faced with a conflict of duties: duty to my country, and duty to my integrity. I am prepared to suffer for my country, but not to cause suffering for it. The burden of suffering in the world is too staggering for me to add to it. I can do little to subtract from it, but that little I will do.

1943

Yesterday afternoon I heard Winston Churchill announce the fall of Singapore. Yesterday afternoon I named my home Fort Juniper. For over a year I have hunted playfully for a name. Yesterday I found the name and at the same time I found my need for the name. The name reminds me of the reality behind the name. My home is my fort in my fight against obstacles that besiege me. Like the juniper I have dug in here and am trying to endure. The juniper teaches me to keep close to the ground. This winter I have come to see what *it* stands for. I have taken it as my coat of arms.

March 13, 1943

During my months in the army, I sometimes made believe there were invisible marchers among the men of my platoon—Whitman, for instance, with his long ambling roll and Thoreau of a straight-ahead motion and always half a step ahead of me. Whitman, I remembered, had known army life; and of Thoreau it was said (was it by Emerson?) that there was something military in his manner. My mind would go back too to far earlier times and bring Socrates in his sandals beside me. I could not picture his manner of walking very well except to know that it was sturdy and untiring. What made him so welcome a companion was knowing that he too had been a soldier and a good one, and that he could be a soldier and Socrates at the same time.

1943

March 18

Within a year and a half three old ladies, in whose homes I once lived and whom I often visited in later years, have died. Mrs. Hopkins went in December of 1941; Mrs. Boynton, in October, 1942; and Miss Dana only the other day, March, 1943.

It is hard to think of old people whom we have long known as dead. The habit of living was so deeply-seated with them that it seems strange that the habit could be broken. The older they grew, the more individual and unforgettable they became. Something has happened to them to be sure: they are gone. But it is easier to think of them as having moved to another street or living in a neighboring town.

April 13

When we came to South Amherst in 1927, Cecil Jewett was already an old man, "a Father-Time-like sort of man," long beard, large nose, wide-brimmed straw hat. Today, sixteen years later, he still lives, and still lives alone in a deserted-looking house. The other day I saw the man himself, or rather a figure so aged, so slow, so seemingly magnified that he was less man than apparition. He was dressed in heavy black coat and great cap and galoshes, and he carried a heavy staff.

1943

Old Man Feeding Hens

The oldest-looking man, the slowest-moving,
I ever saw, dressed all in somber black
And with a great December-snowdrift beard,
Leans on a staff and with his other hand
Feeds a few Barred-Rock hens from a slung basket.

Neither the man nor hens make any sound
For me to overhear. One might suppose
That he had passed beyond the need of words,
Either to speak them or to hear them spoken,
And that his hens had grown into his silence.

The house beside him is a Barred-Rock gray
With not one window-sign of habitation.
Some day and soon it will have less than none,
And on that day the hens may not be fed
Till noon or evening or the second morning.

1943

April 23

The poetry reading went off as well as I have ever had one go. In other respects the day has been memorable. I drove the truck alone up town and got two and a half tons of feed. In the afternoon I unloaded the whole of it on my back. I killed a hen for the first time in my life.

May 27

I keep a Memorial Week rather than one Memorial Day. The last week in May brings my mother's birthday (May 24th) and my father's deathday (May 28th). For me all these white blossoms—shadbush, hawthorne, apple, and pear—are for them.

June 6

I have a new book of poems, *The Sound I Listened For*. I am both author and publisher. Having knocked on the doors of New York and Boston in vain, I decided that if a book could be written in Amherst it could also be published there.

The printing was done in Northampton by the Kraushar Press.

The book is dedicated to Father and is formally published on his birthday, June 8th.

I planned the little book carefully, and had the satisfaction of having it exactly as I wanted it.

1943

July 15

What some people have done with the little book I gave them.

A college English professor took it to class and read the *Seagull* poem to his students. A high school English teacher took her copy to school and read several poems to her scholars. She had them write "reviews" of the book, and sent me several of them. An Episcopal clergyman took the book to church and read the *Juniper* poem to his congregation. A radio man asked permission to read six poems over the radio. A newspaper woman promised to review the book for her newspaper. The director of a writers' conference took the book sufficiently to heart to give me an invitation to visit the conference as its guest.

A woman took the book to the hospital to read during convalescence. A man on his way to visit a friend took the book to read on the train. At the friend's house the book was read aloud at table by various members of the family. A woman lent her copy to neighbors who asked to borrow it. In one case two friends, and in two cases, two sisters, read the book together. A number of people procured additional copies to send to friends. And a good friend of mine, a young man who is studying the dance with the high priestess of that art in this country, took the book to the studio and showed her the *Seagull* poem.

1945

June 17, 1944

Once again, after a long interval, my journal.

Wade Van Dore showed me some experimental verses of his the other day. He asked me if I had done anything experimental. I told him that every poem was experimental.

June 4, 1945

So far as I know, I am free to go on living here at Fort Juniper as long as I go on living. Free to go on with my career. Free to go on living.

September 30

I continue to find new resources in my house. It took me several years fully to learn the value of a roof. A roof is not merely for shelter; it is for elevation, view, sunshine and starlight, as my newly-built "sky porch" testifies.

I am also learning the versatility of my fireplace. Two years ago it proved an almost perfect indoor pen for my hen, Gladys. Today I put my radio in the fireplace and gained a new resonance in the music. With the radio there, one can also hear the music from the roof.

1945

If I could do with my life what I am doing with my house . . .

October 12

This morning I happened to look out and see three mottled cows running along the road, followed by three calves, and they in turn followed by a man and three boys carrying sticks, all ten animals trotting along at about the same pace through the rain and autumn foliage. Moving day for the pasture. The moving time of year—transition, change.

November 4

. . . This book *(We Fly Away)* is based solidly on my own experience and observation. Indeed that experience was almost too solid to start with: it bounded me helpfully, but it also restricted and bound me. It took me nine years to find the freedom of my material. During that time I could not get beyond what I *remembered* my chief character to have said. When I got so I could *predict* what she would have said in other circumstances, I was free to go ahead.

November 15

After five days of rain, mist, and drizzle, I sat and lay for two hours this afternoon in the tingling sunlight. I was indoors, but since I had removed a window, there was nothing between me and the sun. A cold wind was blowing from the northwest, but not on me.

Part of the technique of living is to keep in the sun. For the warm half of the year I have a sky porch; for the cold half I have a removeable window.

December 2

When Princess Juliana of the Netherlands and her husband were entertained by President and Mrs. Ham of Mount Holyoke, Mrs. Ham was half a moment late in going out to greet the party upon their arrival in front of the house. Seeing an unidentified man standing there, she turned to him and asked bluntly, "Who are you?" "Why, my dear," said Mr. Ham slightly horrified, "this is the Prince." Thereupon Mrs. Ham, taking the bull by the horns, asked, "Well, why don't you look like a prince?" It was a triumph of Emersonian self-assertion and imperturbability.

January 3, 1946

It always touches me when Harvard University comes to me for funds. . . .

My vegetarian friends are never pacifist, and my pacifist friends are never vegetarian. The vegetarians accept the necessity of that wholesale slaughter called war; and the pacifists accept the necessity of that wholesale murder

1946

known as the meat industry. The pacifists quote the Bible to prove that it is right to eat animal food. The vegetarians quote the Bhagavat-Gita to prove that men must fight.

In front of me is a small copy of Edward Hicks' early American painting, "The Peaceable Kingdom." The lion and the ox are posing together, and the lamb and the leopard lie peacefully side by side. The leopard, though seemingly made of calico, wears a worried look like that of an elderly librarian who has just heard whispering in the library.

Outdoors, in front of my house, the tree sparrows are feeding on the cracked wheat that I have scattered for them. There is enough wheat for all, and room enough for all. But the tree sparrows are trying to drive one another away.

March 11

. . . I suspect a few of my friends think I have shot my mark, had my spree, and now will peter out. Most of them probably assume that I will go along as I have done, turning out a book of short poems every few years. But a few of them, I think, expect great things of me. They take into consideration the factor of growth. They think I have already grown in my art, and they want me to keep on. They are willing to bet that I will. Whenever I come across

1946

that spirit in a friend, I am suddenly aware that I too am one who is betting on myself.

March 14

Somewhere in his conversations with Eckermann, Goethe speaks of having written some verses without afterwards changing a single word, since, he says, he took pains to put down only what would remain. It's a modified form of the old notion of verbal inspiration. A purer form of it is when the poet puts down, not what he considers carefully, but whatever comes into his head—and doesn't change that. My way of writing poetry is far different. I admit something that might be called inspiration, but it comes in little fragments all mixed up with hard work. I go at a poem in exactly the way a sculptor goes at a clay modeling.

April 4

I have learned something today: that there is abundance of firewood—driftwood—all about me that I can burn in my fireplace and keep me warm. And I have needed it today. These dry, brittle relics of trees lie about the pasture with nothing to do but rot. I salvage them, break them across my knee, and bring them to my hearth. They flatter my thrift. More than that, they make me feel almost as if fed by ravens. I shall have use of them too in summer when my outdoor hearth and iglu is made. Free wood will bake my soybeans.

1949

November 26

Critical readers of my poetry notice first the influences. Then they notice certain qualities of style. After that they observe—or fail to observe—the total form of a poem, its structure and organization. Last of all—if at all—they become aware of what I am saying, the passionate core of meaning.

December 22, 1949

Leslie Cromack, who has the last farm in Amherst on the East Leverett Road, stopped in this afternoon with his five-year-old grandson to see if he could buy a book of my poems for his wife to give his mother for Christmas. He had forgotten the title, but he understood that there was some personal touch about it, some reference perhaps to red barns. (Little he guessed how personal the touch was.)

In July, 1937, a day or two after I had moved into the old house by the brook, Cromack came to mow the field of hay across the road. His quiet mastery of his horses, his nice adaptation of means to ends, his gentle understatement of strength led, months later, to the poem, "The Sound I Listened For," published first in the Virginia Quarterly Review, and later the title poem of both the 1943 and 1944 volumes. In those years I sometimes

1949

thought I should give him a copy of the book, but I never even let him know that he was in the poem. Until today.

After explaining that all three of my books of poems were out of print and hard to get and that I had only one copy (my own much worn one) of *The Sound,* I told him about the paper-covered volume and how it contained most of the same poems. I handed him the book as a gift. Did he know—of course he wouldn't know—that one of the poems was about him, the poem that gave its title to the volume?

Tears came to his eyes. He protested that he hadn't come begging. Taking the book in his hand he asked if I would autograph it. After various questions, I proposed the following inscription:

> For Mary Cromack
> from her son Leslie
> whose voice the poet
> listened for

The tears were more abundant now. He took out his handkerchief and blew his nose. "Getting old," he murmured. "Getting soft."

1949

The Sound I Listened For

What I remember is the ebb and flow of sound
That summer morning as the mower came and went
And came again, crescendo and diminuendo,
And always when the sound was loudest how it ceased
A moment while he backed the horses for the turn,
The rapid clatter giving place to the slow click
And the mower's voice. That was the sound I listened for.
The voice did what the horses did. I shared the action
As sympathetic magic does or incantation.
The voice hauled and the horses hauled. The string of
   one
Was in the other and in the strength was no impatience.
Over and over as the mower made his rounds
I heard his voice and only once or twice he backed
And turned and went ahead and spoke no word at all.

1950

December 26

The fall that I was in the army I happened to see a notice of the publication of Aldous Huxley's *The Art of Seeing,* and asked Mother to give it to me for Christmas. She did. But it is only now, seven years later, that I am thoroughly reading it and putting into practice its theories and exercises. For four days I have not touched my glasses, the same pair that were made for me that year I was in the army, to take the place of some I had just broken. With tinted lenses, too, shutting out for seven years (and how much longer before that I do not know) part of the healing and illuminating power of the sun.

December 30

The Italian Volta, the German Ohm, the French Ampere, and the English Watt—what a parable in international cooperation!

January 3, 1950

This afternoon, after the rain had stopped but while the landscape was still dim with fog and winter, I walked up through the pasture and woodland to the old chestnut. Partly because everything was washed and glistening, partly because I had no dimming glass before my eyes, and partly perhaps because of the very softness of the

1950

light, I enjoyed a constant revelation of color. Never before had the gray-green reindeer moss seemed so luminous, or the silver and violet sheen over the junipers more conspicuous.

January 7

Early morning. A little colder after much warm weather and rain. Snow falling in soft small pellets. Can't quite decide whether or not I hear it fall.

April 14

Yesterday morning we were surprised to find a white world outdoors. It snowed all day, and apparently all night, for this morning the trees are bending under the snow and it is still snowing. I have to make a slight effort to accept and enjoy this unseasonal beauty, for it has interrupted my gardening. But it doesn't take much reflecting to make me feel how this snow is a last beautiful gesture of winter, like Goethe's lyrics in his old age. I am glad that though it is time for winter to be dead and buried, it can still express itself with (delicate) vigor.

May 22

Two days ago Robert Frost, with Armour Craig, called on me on the day before he returned to Cambridge after his month in Amherst. It was the first time I had seen him this spring. It was the first time he had seen my house. He expressed approval of everything indoors and out. My

1950

wild apple tree was at the height of bloom and loaded. Looking at it from indoors, he said the sticks of the window improved the tree—that was what art did. Outdoors he said the fringed polygala was trying to be not a bird but an airplane. Later observation on my part confirmed the felicity of the comparison.

We discussed again Mark 4:1-12, to which he refers in his poem "Directive." At first he maintained that Jesus had said it and meant it, and that he (Frost) agreed. Namely, not merely the fact that some people were for one reason or another excluded, but that they needed to be and ought to be excluded. Later he said with a twinkle: "I know why I brought that into the poem. I wanted to say that it was as good a passage as any other that people wish were not in the Bible." I said, "Ah, that is a good reason. That is the sort of reason I would expect from you."

July 17

Today has been the day I wrote the poem "Squash in Blossom." This morning over an outdoor cup of coffee I made my tentative start. Later, at the white table under the pine, I brought the first draft to completion. I made a few changes, here and there, during the afternoon. After supper I took it to the pitch pine grove on the mound beyond the pasture across the road. But the first stanza didn't get its revisions until I had sat in the white chair outdoors in the dark for some time. Several times I went indoors to my typewriter, and then outdoors again.

1950

Squash in Blossom

How lush, how loose, the uninhibited squash is.
If ever hearts (and these immoderate leaves
Are vegetable hearts) were worn on sleeves,
The squash's are. In green the squash vine gushes.

The flowers are cornucopias of summer,
Briefly exuberant and cheaply golden.
And if they make a show of being hidden,
Are open promiscuously to every comer.

Let the squash be what it was doomed to be
By the old Gardener with the shrewd green thumb.
Let it expand and sprawl, defenseless, dumb.
But let me be the fiber-disciplined tree

Whose leaf (with something to say in wind) is small,
Reduced to the ingenuity of a green splinter
Sharp to defy or fraternize with winter,
Or if not that, prepared in fall to fall.

1952

August 19

Yesterday I took the manuscript of my fourth volume of poems, *The Face Against the Glass,* to the printer Newell. Like the 1943 edition of *The Sound I Listened For,* this is to be a small paper-covered volume issued under my own auspices. Again I have cut the Gordian Knot.

November 7

How does the poet progress in his career? His progress to almost everyone except himself is imperceptible and to himself it is not always clear. He has sold slightly over half the edition of 300 of his book *The Face Against the Glass.* Almost the only recognition has been the reprinting of two of the poems in the N.Y. Times. Locally the little book is little mentioned, and when mentioned, merely mentioned. Almost no one in town has expressed an opinion of the whole collection; and no one in town has praised the collection as a whole.

Still I have my invitations. My first appearance as a character to be written about is in this month's *Yankee.*

August 3, 1952

Ever since the summer of 1926 when I began, consistently, to write poetry, I have known that nothing else I did was more absorbing or seemed more important at the

1952

time of doing. Yet it was not until 1936 when my first book of poems was published that I could endure being called a poet. And up till almost the present day I have preferred to be known as a writer (prose and poetry) rather than simply as a poet. I have resisted letting poetry become central in my life—except during the hours when I was actually writing or trying to write it. Instead of letting poetry suffer the stresses and strains of all my experience, I have let it stay about as it has been and used prose to express whatever poetry did not seem suited for. But I have had a change of mind recently. I am now trying to devote myself to poetry as unstintedly as mystic to God or as lover to beloved.

I am poor, I am unpublished, I am obscure. If I devote myself to what is most important (to me and to others) to do, my poverty and obscurity will not greatly trouble me, will not perhaps seem like failure at all. It is not that prose is ignoble or unimportant; it is only that poetry is nobler and more important. And more difficult. Since the likelihood of winning any of the prizes is small, I might as well aim at the great targets.

August 17

The Jones library is exhibiting a large group of photographs of Amherst men taken years ago by Professor Frank Waugh. Some are notables, some are village characters, and others are men who have not the achievement of the one or the eccentricity of the other, yet have, to the eye at least, as much character as any.

1952

Two of the portraits are labeled "poet," and I am one of the two. It gives me something of a start and also a satisfaction to be summed up in one word. I submit to the label. I am enough of a poet to be called a poet. Some day I may be more poet still.

August 18

It not infrequently happens here at Fort Juniper that a whole day goes by without my speaking to a single soul. This has been true for years, perhaps oftener in winter than in warm weather. Two such days a week ago, Saturday and Sunday, occurred together. And three occurred together this week-end just past. Three days and a half actually, for I spoke to no one until early afternoon today when the girl came with the eggs.

Such spells of social silence are all to the good. I do not forget people nor do they forget me. If my solitude is the warp of my life, people are the woof. I have no desire to make them less, and I couldn't even if I had the desire. When alone I have the freedom of my friends, and am not captured by those who happen to be here.

August 27

When we are young we are like actors in stock: one role this week, another role next. At least we assume that we will have or could have a variety of roles. Later, by choice or force of circumstance or both, we settle down to one role, interminable like a Broadway record run. The choice

1952

then is not whether to do something else, but how well we will do what we are doing.

September 1

. . . A friend was here for supper this evening. Though it was a simple meal, I rejoice that it gave rich evidence of the productivity of my vegetables, herbs, and fruits. We had squash, green beans, and tomatoes from my garden. The potato salad was flavored with my parsley and basil. Some of my beets were served marinated in tarragon vinegar from my tarragon. Elderberry jelly which I made recently was tinctured with some of my thyme. For dessert we had a rhubarb shortcake made from my rhubarb flavored with my spearmint. Freedonia grapes from my vines were on the table at the close of the meal. Thus a very poor man can play the almost-munificent host.

September 6

. . . It was a good evening, for I also wrote several letters and worked a bit on poetry. I played my violin. I went out for a glimpse of the bright full moon, and found a large toad, glistening with dew and moonlight, on my stone doorstep. Around ten o'clock I was ready to go to bed. But a poem about the American eagle, which had been in the back of my mind for years, began to stir. I thought it would be nice to go to bed with the satisfaction of having put down a few tentative lines.

When I looked at my watch . . .

1952

October 1

Anne Blair of Springfield wrote me the other day that when her "beloved Robert Taft" lost the presidential nomination she wrote to him quoting most of my poem "Monadnock."

1952

Monadnock

If to the taunting peneplain the peak
Is standpat, relic, anachronism,
Fossil, the peak can stand the taunt.

There was a time the peak was not a peak
But granite and resistant core,
Something that refused to wear

Away when time and wind and rivers wore
The rest away. Here is the thing
The nervous rivers left behind.

Endurance is the word, not exaltation.
Two words: endurance, exaltation.
Out of endurance, exaltation.

1952

She [Anne Blair] also said that my poem "Portrait" (which she does not know has been referred to T. S. Eliot) was "perfect for Herbert Hoover."

1952

Portrait

Infinite learning, spiritual malaise
Of which as many phases as the moon's,
And universal critical acclaim
Conspire to bring him on the verge of age
To something verging on humility.
Having embraced the heresies one by one
He can afford now to affirm the faith
At no cost to his intellect or renown.
Having exhausted subtlety, he now
Would be plain-spoken, almost, on occasion.
Like a cold peak he rises out of mists
Which he once loved and, moonlit, still might love.
Or like an aging king secure enough,
Weary enough and proud enough to slight
His robes and humor some old dressing-gown.

1952

October 6

My attitude toward my poverty is something of a paradox. I regard it as a liability and try to lessen it, and at the same time regard it as an asset and try, in Thoreau's phrase, to cultivate it. Thus far I have had no actual choice about the poverty itself; I remain poor whatever my attitude.

At its best poverty is a game and an art. At its hardest, it is a price to pay for something worth paying for. And the price may be an incidental price or an essential one. I mean, there are some things I enjoy in spite of being poor, and others because I am poor.

Seldom do I feel poor. What I am rich in, and could be still richer in, outweighs what I am poor in.

October 12

This afternoon at twenty minutes to three I heard outdoors a distant, soft, strange yet half-familiar yapping, and looking up, saw two wedges of wild geese flying high through the cloudless blue. As I watched, the two wedges joined forces and became one. In that long thin flickering line they flew, until the line was nothing but a shimmer.

October 26

I was outdoors washing windows about three o'clock Thursday afternoon, the 23rd, when a car drew in off the road. Wishing to finish the window I was working on, I

1952

did not look to see who it was. In a few moments the car drove away, but someone was coming toward the house. I started down to meet him. It was Robert Frost.

Before going in, we strolled about for a few minutes. He wanted to know where my boundary line ran, remarked on the variety of my trees, and asked if I had been troubled with the white pine weevil. When he saw that some of my pines had been attacked and that I had removed only the vertical shoot, he advised that I take off four of the whorl of five shoots just below to leave a single leader and insure a single-trunk tree. Did I know that the white pine, our finest tree, had been one cause of the American Revolution, since the colonists resented the king's claim to all the best pines for masts for his ships?

A dead female mantis, which I had found that morning, lay on a chair. Frost surprised me by the interest he took in the insect. He asked no end of questions—what they ate, how they wintered, etc. Hearing of their cannibalism, he told me I was fond of them because they showed so vividly what it was in nature I didn't like. I said my attitude was somewhat ambivalent: I gave them every care and consideration, but I stopped at supplying them with food. They had to forage for themselves.

As we started in, Frost noticed my house needed painting and said so. He was surprised to hear it had been painted twice in its twelve years. He said he had often thought of building himself but never had, though an addition he had put on his house in Vermont was about the size of my house.

We looked at my collection of mantis shells, egg-cases, and mantis mummies. It was with a reference to the mantids that he began to discuss my poems. "They are like your interest in the mantis: there are always two things there." He started to say, "Where will you find any—" but checked himself with the remark that he would not compare me to anybody else, but that my poems were good. "I like them for so many different reasons. And always have." He said I was a philosopher, and referred to some sort of indignation in my poetry. I have forgotten the qualifying word. Said my satire had sting. Mentioned "The Two Lords of Amherst" and "Picasso and Matisse" by title.

As to why the editors rejected me so often, Frost professed not to know, then tried to guess. Was it because the poems were too lean, too tight, too dry for them? Did the editors want more juice? Did they fail to feel the emotion in my paradoxes (which Frost felt that I felt)? Did I possibly repeat the good-evil paradox too often? If these were the reasons, there really wasn't much I could do about it. . . .

I said I had hoped he would tell me which poems to throw out. Oh, if that was what I wanted, he said, he might keep the poems longer, say till his return in spring. (When he left, he took the manuscript volume with him.)

April 7, 1953

A year ago I was in hiding. Having been rebuffed in every creative effort, I wanted most of all to withdraw into myself for clarification and renewed strength. So I

1953

had my telephone disconnected, and, night after night, made myself incommunicado and invisible in my bedroom, where, luxuriating in complete spiritual and physical solitude, I read and wrote and thought.

This year the situation is quite different. I am not being rebuffed. Doors have opened and are opening. My aim is to cooperate with what is cooperating with me. . . . The most recent boon came today—forty dollars as a free-will gift from Mrs. Roberts of The Lyric, in reply to my explanation that I could not afford not to sell poems that might be sold. Forty dollars out of the blue to bring me wholly out of the red. . . .

April 23

This afternoon I heard someone coming up to my door whistling. It was a Fuller Brush man.

"Is the lady of the house in?" he asked.

"No," I said, "she is not in."

"We don't often catch them in," he said. "But I want to leave her this little brush."

"Oh, thank you," I said, taking the gift.

"When would she probably be in?" he inquired.

"That is hard to say," I answered truthfully.

"Just like my wife," he said. "And here is a comb for you." He went whistling down the path.

A few days ago I had an offer of marriage (by mail) from a woman in Oklahoma. She has been reading my

1953

Monitor essays for several years, and writing to me frequently and familiarly, without any encouragement from me. I think she thinks I am coy, or need to be awakened. And the longer I don't write—year after year—the more convinced she seems to be that all that needs to be done is for her to keep writing. She grows more and more ardent as I grow more and more silent.

June 17

All my life I have been deficient in power. I mean the power of the ordinary man. The boy's power of fist. The youth's power of love. The young man's power of winning a wife, and of producing and bringing up children. The power of a recognized job, of a place in the community, of money, of driving a good car.

And yet, in spite of deficiencies, I do have power of a sort, and that power grows. I need to keep aware of it and to use it.

July 5

Yesterday I made up a sort of financial confession, copies of which I can send (with or without accompanying checks) to people asking me to contribute to worthy causes. Here it is.

If it is becoming for the asker of a gift to explain why he asks it, it may also be becoming for the man asked to explain why and what he gives or does not give.

As an independent and unpopular writer, I enjoy many rewards, but money is not among them. My income for

1953

1952 was $489.40. For the first six months of 1953 it has been $299.80 (to which gifts totaling $50 may be added). At the moment my checking balance is $27 and my saving balance between $80 and $90. Though I escaped the income tax last year, I never escape the property tax, which this year is $70.50.

Though I live far below The American Standard of Living, I am not impoverished or pitiful. All bills (except the property tax) are paid to date. I own my small home. I am well nourished and adequately clothed. Few writers have more propitious conditions under which to write.

But to live solvently and happily on so little money demands strict economy. I have no car, but depend on walking when I go to town three and a half miles distant. I buy almost no new clothing. I do my own washing, ironing, and mending. I care for my house and prepare my own meals. With the soy bean as a chief protein food, I eliminate absolutely the eating of bird, beast, and fish. I have a garden of vegetables, herbs, and small fruits. To one to whom everything in life is entertaining, it is no hardship to spend no money on "entertainments."

If I had more, I would give more. If I earned more, I would have more. If the earning of more did not mean the losing of still more, I would earn more.

But though I would like to give more, I cannot help wondering whether many good causes today are not too dependent on money. I recall President Conant's appeal for the $5,000,000 endowment for the Harvard Divinity School. The need, he explained, was due "in part to world conditions, in part to the realization of moral laxity at home." There you have it: moral laxity in one hand and five million dollars in the other. So far as I know, the Christian religion made its way in the early days without benefit of modern promotional methods.

July 6

Though I have always known the first names of my four grandparents, clearly I have not felt those names. For whenever I have encountered those names in other people—Daniel and Christy Anne, Oliver and Harriet—I have not thought of my grandparents. In reading the Book of Daniel I have not thought of my grandfather Francis. My Aunt Harriet's name has never been associated in my mind with my grandmother Allen. Two of the principal characters in Santayana's *The Last Puritan* are Harriet and Oliver, but it is only now that I tell myself that those are the names of my mother's parents.

The Santayana book is proving a rich experience for me, beyond the richness of the novel itself. Santayana himself as well as his people in the book touch me in all sorts of ways. Boston, Harvard, poetry, philosophy. The year that this great novel was published (1936) was the year of my first book of poems; and in reviewing it for the Monitor someone said it was as if the Last Puritan had written it.

July 7

Sitting in my grove near my stone man this morning, I thought of my father's name: Ebenezer. Why had I not

1953

felt it more and incorporated it in my own life? Stone of Help. And by a later meaning, Dissenter's Chapel. Didn't I know the helpfulness of a stone? And wasn't my Fort Juniper a sort of Dissenter's Chapel?

1953

Hallelujah: A Sestina

A wind's word, the Hebrew Hallelujah.
I wonder they never give it to a boy
(Hal for short) boy with wind-wild hair.
It means Praise God, as well it should since praise
Is what God's for. Why didn't they call my father
Hallelujah instead of Ebenezer?

Eben, of course, but christened Ebenezer,
Product of Nova Scotia (Hallelujah).
Daniel, a country doctor, was his father
And my father his tenth and final boy.
A baby and last, he had a baby's praise:
Red petticoat, red cheeks, and crow-black hair.

A boy has little say about his hair
And little about a name like Ebenezer
Except that he can shorten either. Praise
God for that, for that shout Hallelujah.
Shout Hallelujah for everything a boy
Can be that is not his father or grandfather.

But then, before you know it, he is a father
Too and passing on his brand of hair
To one more perfectly defenseless boy,
Dubbing him John or James or Ebenezer
But never, so far as I know, Hallelujah,
As if God didn't need quite that much praise.

But what I'm coming to—Could I ever praise
My father half enough for being a father

1953

Who let me be myself? Sing Hallelujah.
Preacher he was with a prophet's head of hair
And what but a prophet's name was Ebenezer,
However little I guessed it as a boy?

Outlandish names of course are never a boy's
Choice. And it takes time to learn to praise.
Stone of Help is the meaning of Ebenezer.
Stone of Help—what fitter name for my father?
Always the Stone of Help however his hair
Might graduate from black to Hallelujah.

Such is the old drama of boy and father.
Praise from a grayhead now with thinning hair.
Sing Ebenezer, Robert, sing Hallelujah!

1953

November 26

For Thanksgiving dinner today I had the same family group here that I had last year: Mother and Father and Ruth and my four grandparents. Their pictures stood on the dining table.

Over the table was a blue cloth. For decoration I had arranged a large golden orange, three golden (a different golden) ears of corn, and sprays of bittersweet.

1953

The menu

Baked soybeans in tomato sauce with fresh basil [1]
Creamed potato with fresh parsley [2]
Mashed squash [3]   Creamed onions
Carrot sticks [4]   Wild grape jelly [5]
Fresh hot brownbread [6]   Milk
Indian tapioca pudding [7]   with cream
Elderflower wine [8]   Salted peanuts

(1) From my indoor herb garden
(2) From my outdoor garden
(3) Could have been from my summer garden
(4) From my winter garden
(5) October 6, 1954
(6) Steamed that morning
(7) Baked the day before
(8) Summer, 1954

1953

After dinner and a short nap I went out and dug up three small pine trees and planted them near my drive-in to provide future screening from the road. Then I moved my Taylor raspberry bushes to the plot that had the corn last summer.

It is now between seven and eight in the evening. Except for such conversation as I had at dinner, I have spoken to no one or been spoken to by no one all day.

November 27

On January 23rd, 1916, when I was fourteen and a half years old and half-way through my freshman year of high school, I began to keep a diary. What started me was the gift from Father of a set of small black-covered blank books, 2½ by 4¾ inches, a book for each month and a page for each day. My rule was to fill each day's page with that day's doings. From January 23rd to the close of the school year on June 23rd, my entries give a revealing, if naive, picture of the boy I was during that first year of high school. A more earnest, conscientious chap it would have been hard to find, concerned above all with his religious duties, his school assignments, his violin practicing, and his health.

The diary begins with a religious dedication of self, and there is hardly a day following that does not contain some pious resolve. As a Comrade of the Quiet Hour, I was pledged to spend fifteen minutes daily in Bible reading and prayer, and my diary tells when I kept my promise and when I failed. On Sundays I went to church once or

1953

twice, to Sunday school, and to Christian Endeavor, where I regularly testified, prayed, worked on various projects, and finally led meetings and was elected recording secretary. I sometimes persuaded my less religious pals to attend a meeting. On one Sunday I tell of having attended six religious services that day. Often I went to Thursday night prayer meeting.

Judging from the diary, school consisted chiefly of tests and grades. Though my day-to-day marks sometimes fell below standard, the grades at the end of each marking period were the highest—a straight A record, which I was to keep up till graduation three years later.

Military drill, which I think was compulsory, was the nearest I came to an extra-curricular activity. I took part in Prize Drill, in Field Day, in the Memorial Day parade, and in a brief escort of militia on their way to Mexico.

One of the captains in the battalion was a senior named Polsey. He was my idol, and I referred to him always as Capt. Polsey. One morning I was *elated* by the privilege of walking to school with him.

In the interests of health I kept sending away for books and pamphlets: on deep breathing, on how to have strong arms, and on the physical culture of the face. The climax was a wrestling course given by mail by Farmer Burns. This necessitated Mother's buying a quantity of khaki cloth to be made into a wrestling mat when stuffed with hay. I had a bar up in one place or another to practice chinning on. I was concerned with getting to bed early each night so that I could get up early enough in the morning to

1953

have my before-school program. How tall I was at the time I do not know, but I weighed 114½ pounds.

It surprises me a little to learn how much of a walker I already was. I walked to the Mystic Lakes, to the Brooks Estate, and to the Lawrence Tower in Middlesex Fels, sometimes with Father, occasionally with a boy, but as often as not, alone. Generally I walked the mile to school, and thought nothing of covering most of that distance again to the library.

Of the books I took out of the library, the one that excited me the most and made the deepest impression was *Power of Will*. Another that I liked was *Have You A Strong Will?* A book I borrowed with pleasure from a schoolmate was *How to Memorize*.

Another surprise to me now is how often I tried my hand at writing. My major achievement was a poem on war—who's to blame?—in nineteen quatrains. I have it in another blank book I kept that year, together with a few shorter poems and several brief prose exhortations. At one time or another I had ideas for greater things, but never got actually started on them, as well as I can remember—a short story to be called "The Bomb Thrower," a book called *Vital Questions,* another book, *God's Peace*, and a musical composition, "Dance of the Jipsies(sic)."

In this same book I put down my "rules and regulations," religious, physical, musical, and intellectual. Each day during 1916 I checked off in little squares the rules that I had obeyed.

There is evidence, too, that I had considerable fun and

1954

recreation that year. I went skating, played ball, and played a little tennis. I went to three concerts in Boston, to several movies at Tremont Temple, and was taken by Ruth and George to see Buffalo Bill. The playfulness of my cat Pat gave me much pleasure. My enterprise with tame mice reached its climax this year. Up in our attic I kept many mice of various kinds in elegant cages. I bought, bred, and sold mice, and recorded the birth of each new litter. But even here was duty: I had to feed them daily and clean their cages frequently. "Mice all clean and fed" is a frequent entry. Finally, on April 21st, after several sales, I gave the remainder away to my schoolmate, Arthur Bowden.

During these five months Ruth finished her college career and got a secretarial job in New York. Already she was engaged to George Ehinger. Grandfather and Grandmother made us a long visit, and while there, March 13th, celebrated their golden wedding. And on the 31st of March I put on long pants.

June 28, 1954

Nothing can cure a poet's malaise except to write new poems. He can't live emotionally on his past.

AFTERWORD

The poet's Journal reaches its suspenseful close in 1954; the poet's life, despite his years, is still beginning. That summer Francis was invited to teach a poetry class at the Chautauqua Writer's Workshop, to which he returned the next four summers. This community of writers was "a healthy break in my semi-hermitic life," he wrote in his autobiography. "But if Chautauqua could do this much for me, what would Rome do—a whole year of it?"[1]

Awarded a fellowship in writing by the American Academy, Francis left Amherst in 1957 for a year's residency in the city so many poets have sought. Soon after his arrival at the Academy, he began his explorations of Rome, trying out his newly acquired Italian. He found his way to the graves of Shelley and Keats, to the nunnery where Santayana lived his last years, and to the church of Santa Maria to witness a ceremony on the anniversary of Brother Juniper, "the most amusing and possibly the most saintly of the first followers of St. Francis."

When he returned to Amherst, he found his home, Fort Juniper, unchanged, while he himself was entering a new phase of expansion and recognition. After the publication of his fifth volume of poems, *The Orb Weaver* (1960), he was invited to take part in poetry weekends at Wesleyan and Syracuse, and to be the Phi Beta Kappa poet at Harvard. He travelled to Ireland the next year to visit the

1. THE TROUBLE WITH FRANCIS, University of Massachusetts Press, 1971, p. 110.

Afterword

birthplace of his grandfather Francis, and went on to renew friendships in Italy. The University of Massachusetts Press became his publisher in 1965, publishing in the decade that followed *Come Out into the Sun, Like Ghosts of Eagles, New Poems* (1974), and *Collected Poems* 1936–1976. Readers who knew his work well realized that he had fulfilled his youthful intuition that he might "combine all these things" in his poetry: truth to fact, moral and philosophical commitment, and the freedom of one who has put his trust in imagination.

Born in 1901, Robert Francis has literally lived the life of this century. He has been educated in its sciences, has known its headlong changes, and, as an American, the horror of its wars and its natural and social disasters. Czeslaw Milosz reminds us that a 20th century poet, no less than one writing earlier, "stands before reality that is every day new, miraculously complex, inexhaustible, and [he] tries to enclose as much of it as possible in words. That elementary contact, verifiable by the five senses, is more important than any mental construction."[2] In the light of this definition, poem after poem by Francis comes to mind, in which his remarkable attention to particular beings brings them to life. As *The Dandelion Gatherer*,

> Bulging in petticoats in May she comes
> Barefoot or in old bursting shoes, her hair

---

2. Czeslaw Milosz, THE WITNESS OF POETRY: The Charles Eliot Norton Lectures 1981–82, Harvard, 1983, p. 56.

Afterword

> Bandanna'd and her ears hooped down with gold,
> Bearing a gunnysack with no one knows
> How many thousand martyred golden heads . . . .

Basic to his vision is the understanding that "the very act of naming things presupposes a faith in their existence and thus in a true world."[3.] Among his later poems the naming of familiar things, with wit and skill amounting to magic, gives fresh and dramatic consciousness of them.

> backroad leafmold   stonewall chipmunk
> underbrush grapevine woodchuck shadblow
> —from *Silent Poem*

> Pick any blue   sky-blue   cerulean   azure
> cornflower   periwinkle   blue-eyed grass
> blue bowl   bluebell   pick lapis lazuli
> blue pool   blue girl   blue Chinese vase
> —from *Blue Cornucopia*

The authority which flows like a strong current through these poems is that of a man who, though he chose a protected life, has never sheltered himself from knowledge of the agony and violence of the world. Fort Juniper has been a good "observatory" from which to focus and test his "direct and natural outlook," culminating in a realization of the darkness of the universe.

3. *Ibid.*, p. 57.

Afterword

Across this pessimistic view, of the prevalence of "all that is hostile to human life and its fulfillment," he writes his equally persistent account of individual survival and flourishing. In *The Swimmer*

> Observe how he negotiates his way
> With trust and the least violence, making
> The stranger friend, the enemy ally.
> The depth that could destroy gently supports him.
> With water he defends himself from water.
> Danger he leans on, rests in. The drowning sea
> Is all he has between himself and drowning.
>
> What lover ever lay more mutually
> With his beloved, his always-reaching arms
> Stroking in smooth and powerful caresses?

Experience confirms his belief in the staying power of human values: "truthfulness, justice, courage, mercy, and the virtue of putting the interest of another person above the interest of oneself."[4] The last stanza of his *Dolphin* reaches to an apprehension of what Milosz independently sees as "a new image of the world, still timidly developing."[5]

---

4. Francis, p. 236.
5. Milosz, p. 53.

Afterword

Nothing less than forgiveness dolphins teach us
If we, miraculously, let ourselves be taught.
Enduring scientific torture no dolphin has yet
(With experimental electrodes hammered into its skull)
In righteous wrath turned on its tormentors.
What will science ever find more precious?
The sea relaxes. They bless the sea.

                                Cornelia Veenendaal

Richard Gillman, whose friendship with Robert Francis began almost 40 years ago, is a writer who makes his home in New York state's North Country.

Robert Francis was graduated from Harvard in 1923, published his first volume of poetry in 1936, and received the Shelley Memorial Prize two years later. Thus began a long and distinguished writing career. He held the Golden Rose of the New England Poetry Club in 1942–43 and was Phi Beta Kappa poet at Tufts in 1955 and at Harvard in 1960. In 1957–58 he lived in Rome on a fellowship from The American Academy of Arts and Letters. Ten years later he returned to Italy on an Amy Lowell Travelling Scholarship. In 1974 he received the Brandeis Creative Arts Award; and in 1975 the University of Massachusetts Press established in his honor the Juniper Prize, awarded annually for a previously unpublished original manuscript of poems.

In addition to being the author of eight volumes of poetry, Mr. Francis is the author of four books of prose. He is a Fellow of The Academy of American Poets.

"At last, after a rough passage, there was Innisfree. No hive for the honeybee and no log cabin, but of course I hadn't expected them. They were only in the bee-loud glade of Yeats's stravaiging mind. But the whole island was covered with rowan trees, wearing their red berries like jewels, and the thought suddenly came to me . . . . I'll take back some branches to the poet."

Fairy Tales, Fantasy, Animals
"Only Connect", P. L. Travers

This book was typeset in Baskerville and printed on acid-free paper by Maple-Vail Press at Binghamton, New York.

Rowan Tree Press
124 Chestnut Street
Boston, Massachusetts 02108